The Miracles

THE MIRACLES

Exploring the Mystery of
JESUS'S DIVINE WORKS

SIMON J. KISTEMAKER

BakerBooks
Grand Rapids, Michigan

Published by Baker Books
a division of Baker Publishing Group
P.O. Box 6287, Grand Rapids, MI 49516-6287
www.bakerbooks.com

Printed in the United States of America

Library of Congress Cataloging-in-Publication Data
Kistemaker, Simon.
    The miracles : exploring the mystery of Jesus's divine works / Simon J. Kistemaker.
        p. cm.
    ISBN 10: 0-8010-6607-7 (pbk.)
    ISBN 978-0-8010-6607-8 (pbk.)
    1. Jesus Christ—Miracles. I. Title
BT366.3.K57 2006
232.9′55—dc22   2006005229

Scripture translations in this book are the author's own.

Contents

5

INTRODUCTION

We often use the word *miracle* when someone recovers from a serious injury or a life-saving surgery. In doing so, we express our inability to explain the healing power that is present in the human body. We realize that the recovery is not because of the skill and expertise of surgeons alone but hinges on the innate strength that resides within our physical body and overcomes the odds against restoration.

Nevertheless, we readily admit that a miraculous recovery from injury or infirmity differs from the miracles Jesus performed when he healed the sick and raised the dead. We attribute a return to normal health and strength to a mysterious power that God created within our physical body. But the miracles Jesus did were different because the power to heal and restore people resided in him.

This does not mean that we are fully able to explain Jesus's miracles. All we can do is describe them as we look at his ministry recorded in the Gospels. The evangelists portray him as God's miracle-worker, who healed all diseases and raised people from the dead.

The miracles Jesus executed were placed within a context that pointed to his divinity. After they witnessed these astounding events, the people asked whether Jesus was the Son of David, namely, the Messiah. After cleansing the lepers, Jesus dispatched them to the priests as a testimony that he indeed was the one sent by God. He put the learned teachers of the Law in a quandary by having them choose the easier of two acts that only God could do: to forgive sin or to heal a paralytic. When Jesus told the man to stand up and walk, he proved his divinity.

When Jesus cast out demons, they shouted for everyone to hear that he was the Son of the Most High God. The demons feared that he had come to torment them before their time of punishment. Even though the clergy of Jesus's day refused to acknowledge him as God's Son, the demons trembled in submission to him.

Although the Master healed all those who came to him, when he approached the sick and afflicted he was selective. For instance, only one man at the Pool of Bethesda was healed, but the others languishing at the water's edge were not. In his hometown, Nazareth, Jesus was unable to do many mighty works with the exception of restoring to health a few sick people.

Healing occurred immediately when Jesus spoke or laid his hands on those who suffered. He used different methods, including daubing with mud the eyes of a man born blind and touching the eyes of another. At other times he healed the people at a distance, among them the servant of a Roman centurion, the son of a royal official, and the daughter of a Syro-Phoenician woman.

At least two of Jesus's miracles feature the work or glory of God. In the case of the man born blind, Jesus referred to the work of God displayed in his life. When he was about to raise Lazarus from the dead, Jesus said that the bystanders would see the glory of God. Miracles are not isolated incidents but are meant to reveal the glory of God in his power and might. Hence he is worthy to receive the people's praises of thanksgiving.

What was Jesus's purpose for his healing ministry? The answer is to show that he was the Messiah. John the Baptist sent his disciples to Jesus to ask whether he was "the coming one." Jesus answered that everyone could attest to his messiahship because of the miracles:

- The blind received their sight.
- The lame walked.
- The lepers were cleansed.
- The deaf were able to hear.
- The dead were raised.
- The poor heard the gospel preached.

Only Jesus the Messiah was able to perform these miracles. He proved to be the Son of God sent to set his people free.

Nature Miracles

Turning Water into Wine

John 2:1–11

Jesus and Mary

After meeting John the Baptist at the River Jordan, where Jesus was baptized, he and his disciples traveled to Galilee. The distance could be covered at a brisk walking pace within a few days. They arrived at the village of Cana near Nazareth. Just then the villagers were celebrating a wedding feast at which Mary, Jesus's mother, had agreed to serve the guests.

Weddings were celebrated as real feasts that might continue for seven days. After an engagement period that lasted a year, the actual marriage day began in the evening of the wedding day. Then the bridegroom with his friends went to the house of the bride and brought her accompanied by bridesmaids to his home.

Although the details are sparse, we can confidently assume that the bride or bridegroom was either a friend or a relative of Mary. We do know that Jesus had been invited to come to the feast with his disciples. Undoubtedly the presence

[handwritten margin note: ?]

13

[handwritten note at bottom: ? No evidence for this, and it's irrelevant]

of extra guests at the wedding may have contributed to a shortage of wine as time elapsed.

Wedding feasts were joyous occasions, during which the guests consumed large quantities of food and wine. In Hebrew culture, the consumption of wine was part of entertaining invited guests and enjoying each other's fellowship. This beverage was sometimes diluted with water to keep the alcohol level low. In addition, society's rules made intoxication culturally unacceptable. Indeed Scripture speaks against drunkenness.

As time went by, the servers noticed that the wine supply was diminishing and would run out. This predicament would cause inevitable embarrassment to the bridal couple and family and inescapable financial expense. They had to do something quickly to save the situation and avert social disgrace. Mary seized the moment to enlist the help of Jesus. Of all the guests and servers, she knew him best. And the relationship between Mary and Jesus was firm, especially because he had been her breadwinner after the death of her husband, Joseph.

To our ears Jesus's response to Mary sounds rather brusque. He said, "Woman, what does this have to do with you and me? My time has not yet come." In the Western world it is exceedingly rude and ill-mannered for a son to address his mother as "woman." Not so in Jesus's day, where the word *woman* was a title of respect much the same as the term *ma'am* is a courteous address in the southern part of the United States. The intent of Jesus's address would be similar to "my dear mother."

However, the words Jesus spoke put a distance between him and his mother so she would realize a change had taken place in their relationship. Mary had to acknowledge that Jesus was no longer her breadwinner but now fulfilled the role to which God had called him. The mysterious words, "My time has not yet come," pointed to his impending suffering, death, resurrection, and ascension. Mary had to recall the words spoken by the twelve-year-old Jesus in the temple: "Didn't you know that I must be in my Father's house?"

Jesus turned the intimate relationship of mother and son into that of a sinner in need of a Savior. He had come to earth to save his people from their sins, and Mary had to acknowledge that she too was a sinner for whom Jesus had come as the Messiah. Indeed, as the Lamb of God he would eventually die a cruel death to remove her sin. He made it plain to her that she had no more claim on him than anyone else would have because he was the Son of God, and he had been sent to do his Father's bidding.

Mary had to remember that decades earlier in the temple aged Simeon had spoken words about her son's destiny. He had said that Jesus's life was set for the fall and the rise of Israel and that a sword would pierce Mary's soul too.

Now standing at the beginning stage of that destiny, Jesus alerted his mother to the realization that his earthly ministry had begun. He and not his mother would determine the schedule of this ministry that eventually led to his death on the cross of Calvary.

Then Mary informed the servants to do whatever Jesus told them. She knew that Jesus would be able to tackle the predicament. Six water pots made out of stone stood nearby. They were used by the Jews for ceremonial washings. Each one had the capacity of holding twenty to thirty gallons. Jesus ordered the servants to completely fill all the six pots with water from the well. He wanted to make sure that the containers were empty before they were filled with clean drinking water.

Jesus did not speak any magical formula, did not touch the water, and did not pray to God for a miracle. There was no display of power, no grand gesture of trickery, no sleight of hand. Jesus merely asked one of the servants to draw some of the water from these pots and take it to the headwaiter. And then the miracle of turning water into wine happened.

15

The Mystery

The servants saw that the water had turned into wine. Unable to explain the miracle that had occurred, they went to the headwaiter and presented the wine to him. He tasted the wine, unaware of the miracle, and immediately reacted by telling the bridegroom that something had gone awry. It was customary to serve the good wine first and then that of lesser quality. When the guests had had their fill, they would not be able to tell the difference. But here the reverse had happened, that is, the poorer wine had been served until it was consumed, and then suddenly the better wine became available.

The bridegroom did not know how the good wine had come into the banquet hall. But when he was told that the six water pots were filled with a better-quality wine, he was overwhelmed with the wedding gift Jesus had presented to the bridal couple. The enormous quantity of wine became a fitting wedding present for the newlyweds.

The miracle itself will always remain a mystery to us, for Jesus' supernatural power was at work in changing water into wine. But we are able to understand some aspects of this event, that is, when Jesus performed this miracle he eliminated the element of time. The making of wine takes a long time, which begins with the growing of grapes, then harvesting and squeezing them, and last, collecting the juice. Then the process of fermenting has to take its course. After extra time has elapsed, the wine can be tasted and consumed. It is a known fact that the more time passes, the better the taste of the wine.

Jesus turned water into wine with a miracle that occurred instantaneously. But in effect, the growing process from the tiny blossoms to the full-grown grapes is also a miracle. And so is the fermenting process that works silently and unobtrusively. No human being has the power, knowledge, and ability to duplicate these miracles.

* This is the point!
He is Creator, not bound by
time or anything else.

According to the apostle John, turning water into wine is the first miraculous sign that Jesus performed in Cana of Galilee. Miracles revealed Jesus's glory, but they also fulfilled the purpose of causing his disciples to put their faith in him. As a rule, miracles usually take place to create faith in Jesus or occur in answer to faith. By turning water into wine, Jesus turned his disciples into believers. They were able to verify the truth of his words that they would see heaven opened and God's angels ascending and descending on the Son of Man.

The wedding feast account puts Jesus center stage. We are not told anything about the bridegroom, the bride, the master of ceremonies, or Mary's relationship to the bridal couple. The primary focus in this picture is on Jesus, the miracle-worker. The others are meant to be secondary. Jesus displayed his glory as the one sent by the Father into the world. This sign was the first in a series of miracles that Jesus performed during his ministry.

Points to Ponder

- There is a measure of symbolism in this account. Jesus's presence at the wedding in Cana points to the celestial wedding banquet at the end of time. Then Jesus will be the bridegroom and God's people the bride. Here I see a picture within a picture because the guests at the marriage of the bride will be God's people, and they, in turn, will be the bride of the bridegroom, namely, the Lamb.

- Jesus no longer turns water into wine at weddings, but he wants to be present at a wedding when a husband and a wife start a family. He desires to be the head of every family, the unseen guest at every meal, and the silent listener to every conversation.

17

- Jesus still comes with promises and tells a bridal couple to trust in him with all their heart and not to rely on their own understanding. He urges them to acknowledge him in all that they do and then he will bless them by making their paths straight.

STILLING OF A STORM

Matthew 8:23–27; Mark 4:35–41; Luke 8:22–25

The Tempest

At the end of a busy day of teaching the crowds, Jesus was physically and mentally exhausted. He had healed many sick people along the western shore of the Lake of Galilee and had taught crowds of people during much of the day. With his disciples, Jesus boarded a fishing vessel in the evening. The boat was most likely owned by one of them, perhaps Peter. Jesus told them to head for the other side of the lake to an area the Jews avoided because of its predominantly Gentile population. As they crossed the lake, there were other boats with them as well.

Jesus longed for a period of rest and relaxation. Having found a place in the rear of the boat, he fell asleep almost immediately. Even though he had demonstrated amazing stamina all day long, he now showed that his physical body needed rest. While his disciples propelled the oars and navigated the craft, he slept.

The disciples—many of them were fishermen—were fully familiar with the lay of the land around them as well as with the dimensions and dangers of this body of water. The distance across the lake from west to east is eight miles (thirteen kilometers); it is thirteen miles (twenty-one kilometers) from north to south. As an extension of the River Jordan, the lake is located in a deep trough surrounded by high hills except for a wide stretch at both ends to the north and to the south. While the lake lies far below sea level, it receives its water from the melting snows of nearby Mount Hermon to the north.

During the hot summer months, the temperature at the lake can rise to 100º F (37º C) in the shade. When cool mountain air rushes down toward the hot air above the lake, sudden storms develop and turn its usually calm waters into a violent and dangerous whirlpool. The sudden clash of air masses puts people in mortal danger if they happen to be on the lake when this occurs.

Storm waves of six feet high terrify even the most seasoned fishermen. We can well imagine that this is exactly what occurred on the Lake of Galilee that evening when Jesus had fallen asleep in the stern. A sudden storm descended upon them, but Jesus was sound asleep with his head on a sailor's cushion. He was dead to the world even though a fierce storm was raging all around him. No howling wind, no splashing waves, and no lurching of the boat had any effect on him. Nothing seemed to awaken him.

Nevertheless, when called, he immediately listened to the shouts of his disciples. They cried out to their Lord and Master to save them from a watery grave. Their screams alerted him to the reality that their lives were in danger. They were perishing and needed immediate help. As soon as the disciples cried for help, Jesus instantly woke up. He arose, rebuked the wind, and told the sea to be quiet. All at once the wind died down and the sea became completely calm. The water was smooth as glass.

After that incident Jesus addressed the disciples and asked them why they were afraid. As a fundamental rule, they should have realized that in the presence of their Master they were always safe and secure. Surely the wind and the waves vented their fury against all who were out on the lake, but with Jesus aboard they had nothing to fear. Even so, this called for faith in him. Therefore, Jesus asked them the pointed question, "Where is your faith?" Jesus has never reproved anyone for trusting too much in him. He always pays attention to the childlike faith of his followers.

The disciples were awestruck when they witnessed Jesus's power over the elements in nature. They observed a miracle in the midst of a frightening predicament in which Jesus was completely in charge.

Why did they not realize that with Jesus on board, their boat would never sink? As the agent of creation, he was completely in control of nature's elements. Did they not know that all of creation had to listen to his voice? If they had only known that they had the Creator of the universe on board, they would have been sure of their safety. Jesus was not rebuking them for showing fear but for their lack of faith. Therefore, he taught them the lesson that in the presence of their Master they were always safe and secure.

Jesus' Sovereignty

The disciples were awestruck when they saw Jesus's majestic sovereignty extending over both wind and waves. They asked, "Who is this man? Even the wind and the sea obey him." They had witnessed his ability to conquer nature's forces, which they regarded as the powers of darkness. Their minds went back to Moses, who by extending his hand over the Red Sea parted the waters so the Israelites could safely cross over to the other side. Similarly, in the days of Joshua

21

the waters of the River Jordan stopped flowing so that all Israel could cross over on dry land.

All along they had known that no one but God could control the wind and the tempest. Now Jesus merely spoke to the storm and both wind and water obeyed him. It is true that from their familiarity with nature they knew that storms on the Lake of Galilee could arise and dissipate in a matter of minutes. Nonetheless, amid the howling wind and splashing waves Jesus spoke words of rebuke, and these natural forces instantly became subservient to him. When that miracle occurred, his disciples acknowledged him as the Son of God and Son of Man.

The disciples now saw a display of Jesus's divinity in action. No longer was he the carpenter turned prophet and the teacher who had come from Nazareth. They now realized that he was both divine and human with powers that controlled nature around them. They stood in awe and acknowledged Jesus as their Sovereign Lord. Jesus fulfilled the words of the psalmist who spoke of people going to the sea in ships, of tempests and waves, of sailors crying out to the Lord, and of God stilling the storm to a whisper (Ps. 107:23–30).

Points to Ponder

- If the disciples had known that Jesus was the agent of creation and had power over the forces of nature, they would have let him sleep. He was in need of a well-deserved rest. They should have realized that Jesus would never expose himself and his disciples to the danger of drowning in the Lake of Galilee. But instead of trust and confidence, they lacked faith and were filled with mortal fear.
- Is fear a natural reaction to outside forces? Does fear always demonstrate a lack of faith? Should Christians

ever be afraid? The answer to these questions is that fear indeed drives away faith; conversely, faith abolishes fear. In the Gospels, Acts, and Revelation, Jesus repeatedly tells his people, "Fear not!" He gave his followers this promise, "I am with you to the end of the age" (Matt. 28:20). Whenever we are in a situation that causes fear as a natural reaction, we should remember that fear should drive us to Jesus, not away from him. He always stands next to us and speaks words of encouragement. Jesus sets us free from fear.

- On the other hand, Scripture teaches us to fear God and love him with our heart, soul, and mind. We express godly fear when we live in harmony with his Word and precepts. Fear in the sense of reverence for God is one of the greatest spiritual riches we can ever possess. We revere him as Creator of all things; we know that he is fully in control of every situation, including the tempests of one kind or another that upset our lives.

FEEDING THE FIVE THOUSAND

Matthew 14:13–21; Mark 6:32–44; Luke 9:10–17;
John 6:1–13

Shepherd and Sheep

All four Gospels record the miracle of Jesus feeding five thousand men, not counting the women and the children. If we agree that there are just as many men as there are women, the crowd doubles in size. And if we add children, the total count may well be in excess of twenty-five to thirty thousand people. To feed such a multitude on the spur of the moment is without a doubt a miracle.

The Gospel writers also relate where and when the feeding took place. Jesus and his disciples had gone to a solitary place removed from neighboring towns and villages. It was on the eastern shore of the Lake of Galilee in the spring of the year, probably in April, while the grass was still green. Jesus chose this place to find privacy and be away from the multitudes that followed him wherever he went.

However, the quietness that Jesus and his disciples sought came to an end when people by the thousands approached him. They walked around the lake and came to the place where Jesus was. They wanted him to heal their sick, and they came to be instructed by him.

Jesus spent the rest of the day ministering to the people because they were like sheep without a shepherd. Although the clergy of that day tried to give them spiritual guidance and religious instruction, they failed. Jesus filled that need. He cared for the people with his teaching, and with his deeds he healed the sick and afflicted.

The people stayed until the end of the day. It soon became apparent that they were in need of physical nourishment. The time for teaching the crowds had come to an end, and the time to care for the needs of their physical bodies had arrived. In a sense Jesus became their gracious host while the people were his expectant guests. Would he be able to care for this immense multitude and still remain their supplier?

All the Gospel writers report that the disciples came to Jesus with the suggestion to send the multitudes away so they could buy food in neighboring villages. But Jesus knew exactly what he was going to do. He asked the disciples whether they had the funds to buy sufficient bread for all these people. He wanted them to participate in the work of feeding the crowds, and he tested their faith by instructing them to satisfy the crowds' physical needs.

Philip made a quick calculation and guessed that the amount of money a laborer earned in eight months would not be sufficient to give each person a single bite. He quickly realized the impossibility of meeting the needs of the crowds. His suggestion had been a mere guess, and now he looked to Jesus for help in solving the problem.

Bread and Fish

Andrew, Simon Peter's brother, noticed a boy who had five cakes of barley bread and two small fish. This was sufficient to satisfy a hungry boy but amounted to nothing in front of a crowd. Hence, Andrew questioned Jesus how far this minute quantity of food would go in meeting the needs of a multitude. Andrew failed to realize that he was standing in the presence of the Creator of the universe who daily feeds all his creatures. Furthermore, the disciples failed to see that Jesus never sends people away empty-handed. He always ministers to those who come in full dependence on him.

Barley bread was eaten by the poor who could not afford bread made of better grains. Barley is inappropriate for making cohesive bread; wheat and rye are better-suited grains for that purpose. The two small fish were the size of sardines served as relish when salted. This was Jesus's choice to feed the multitude.

Jesus ordered the disciples to have the people sit down on the green grass in groups of hundreds and fifties. This was done by families, and thus the total number could readily be counted. They were seated in certain divisions in an orderly manner, so that there was no confusion. Heads of families were in charge of gathering their own clans, much the same as Moses grouped the Israelites in the Sinai desert.

Then Jesus took the bread and fish in his hands, looked up to heaven, and blessed the food with thanksgiving to God, the giver of every good and perfect gift. Thus, he showed the people dependence on God to supply their daily needs and the necessity of expressing gratitude.

When Jesus broke the bread, the miracle of multiplication occurred in a manner that cannot be explained to anyone's satisfaction. Questions about this miracle are multiple, but the Scriptures are silent on exactly how the miracle took place. This miracle, however, can be explained by comparing it to the miracle that God performs when on a daily basis he feeds the total population of the earth. Without a doubt, that feat is a miracle!

Jesus gave the bread and the fish to his disciples, who in turn passed it on to the people until all were filled. When everyone was satisfied, he instructed the disciples to gather the leftover pieces of bread and fish so that nothing would be wasted. All the leftover food filled twelve baskets.

This miracle portrays Jesus caring for the spiritual as well as the physical needs of the people. He taught them the Old Testament Scripture and brought them God's revelation. In short, he gave them the bread of life. And at the end of the day he fed them bread and fish to sustain them physically.

Points to Ponder

- God is good to all, for he causes rain to fall on the just and the unjust. Indeed he daily provides food and drink for all people, even though some experience periods of famine. In a few words, this fact in itself is a miracle that demands grateful responses from the recipients.

- At mealtime Christians express their thanks to God and often teach their children to pray, "God is great, God is good, and we thank him for our food." Jesus expressed his thankfulness to God the Father and by his example teaches Christians to express their gratitude to him as well. However, neglect to give thanks is a sign of ingratitude, and a refusal to do so is an act of insolence that results in falling away from the living God.

- The people whom Jesus fed probably thought of the prophet Elijah, whose miracle in Zarephath consisted of the widow's jar of flour never being empty and her jug of oil never running dry (1 Kings 17:7–15). And they remembered that the prophet Elisha fed a hundred men with twenty barley cakes and still had food left over (2 Kings 4:42–44).

- Here in their midst they acknowledged a prophet much greater than either Elijah or Elisha. They saw him as the one Moses had predicted, namely, the Messiah, the Great Prophet. They even wanted to make him their king to overthrow the Roman occupiers. But Jesus would not be a political king in an earthly kingdom. He is King of kings and Lord of lords in a kingdom that is not of this world.

JESUS WALKING ON WATER

Matthew 14:22–33; Mark 6:45–51; John 6:16–21

Slow Boat

After a pleasant evening with relatives or friends, we know the time has come to say good-bye. Then the task of straightening and tidying the rooms and washing the dishes falls to us as gracious host and hostess. Afterward we relax a while before we retire for a night's rest.

In a sense, this is what happened to Jesus and the disciples. After feeding a multitude of five thousand men, not counting women and children, Jesus dismissed the people. He told his disciples to get into the boat and go ahead of him across the Lake of Galilee toward the town of Bethsaida. He himself withdrew and went to a high place to spend time in prayer. He needed time to be alone and commune with his Father. Among other needs, he prayed for the safety and well-being of the disciples who needed his protection from the stormy elements of wind, water, and waves.

It was late in the evening when the disciples entered the boat. As soon as they left the shore, they faced a wind that soon developed into a storm. The disciples were kept from making any noticeable progress. Unable to hoist a sail, they were consigned to ply their oars, but all their manpower appeared to be of little avail. They realized that their progress was minimal, and after many hours of rowing they were no further ahead than the middle of the lake. They were still about three miles from their destination in the waning hours of the night. Tired and frustrated they knew that their exertion had resulted only in limited success.

The disciples wondered why Jesus had sent them out at night alone on the lake. Had he forsaken them? Especially in stormy weather they wanted to hear words of assurance from him; they would welcome his ever-present power over nature. Certainly they wondered where he could be. Was he sleeping while they toiled?

Voicing these questions, they suddenly saw someone walking on the waves of the lake. They had rowed all night long without making substantial progress, and now they saw a faint figure in the distance effortlessly approaching as though to pass them. How could a man walk on the surface of the water as if it were dry ground? Would he not sink and drown? They were filled with fear. Suddenly one of them cried out, "It is a ghost!" All agreed that it was a phantom, a delusive appearance, a demonic spirit floating as an apparition above the surface of the water. They were terrified, and every trace of courage vanished.

Then they heard a familiar voice, the voice of Jesus saying to them, "Take heart, it is I. Don't be afraid." Jesus had not at all abandoned them. He had spent time in prayer, asking his Father to protect them from harm and danger. But now he wanted to strengthen their faith in him by showing them that he controlled the elements. Right in front of them, they witnessed the miracle of Jesus exerting his full power over nature; he was able to defy the laws of gravity and liquidity. The physical forces were fully subject to him.

Faith and Fear

This miracle produced in Peter the reaction Jesus had intended, namely, Peter put his faith in him. He said, "Lord, if it is you, tell me to come to you on the waves." He did not doubt for one moment that the person was Jesus. In fact, because he knew it was Jesus, he asked the Lord whether he might walk with him on the water. His petition was not meant to convey to his fellow disciples that he was stronger in faith than they were. Peter wanted to be next to Jesus so that he too could experience Christ's power over nature. He needed divine approval from the Lord to make this miracle become authentic for him in answer to faith.

As long as Peter looked to Jesus, he indeed could walk on water while winds blew and waves surged. The moment he looked away from the Lord and saw the force of wind and water, he plunged down into the deep. But before he went under, he cried for help. Immediately Jesus took him by the hand and pulled him out of the water. A gentle rebuke came from Jesus's lips, "O you of little faith, why did you waver?" Then both of them came aboard, and the power of the wind stopped at once, to the utter amazement of the disciples. They worshiped Jesus and said, "Truly, you are the Son of God!"

Peter failed to keep looking at Jesus and therefore went down into the water. When he cried out, "Lord, save me!" Jesus took him by the hand and pulled him up into the boat. Notice that Peter's urgent prayer for deliverance was followed by genuine worship.

Jesus walked on water, Peter walked on water, and the wind stopped blowing. What is the significance of this series of miracles? How do we explain these phenomena? We can begin with the feeding of the five thousand, where Jesus demonstrated his power to perform an extraordinary miracle. That should have left an indelible impression on the disciples that, from a human perspective, Jesus could do the

31

impossible. But their minds were dulled because of lack of sleep and their bone-tired limbs. Their hearts were callous and inattentive. In the midst of a storm, weary disciples at the oars failed to apply the meaning of the miracle to their present situation. To be sure, the miracle of Jesus walking on water came unexpectedly at night and in adverse weather conditions.

Jesus called out to the disciples, "It is I; don't be afraid." By uttering the words, "It is I," he took on the identity of God who commissioned Moses to go to the Israelites in Egypt and say, "'I am' has sent me to you" (Exod. 3:14). God revealed himself as the ever-present God who performed miracles among them in Egypt and in the crossing of the Red Sea. Similarly, Jesus walked on the water of the Lake of Galilee and identified himself as divine. His disciples worshiped him as the Son of God, the Messiah.

As the Master of the universe, Jesus could defy the law of gravity because he is the lawgiver and by his divine power he overrules this law. Peter could walk on water because his faith in Jesus enabled him. But when he looked away from Jesus and began to waver, the miracle ended for Peter.

The wind stopped blowing the moment Jesus entered the boat. This phenomenon also occurred at an earlier incident when he stilled the storm on the Lake of Galilee. Now with Jesus aboard, the disciples arrived at the other side in record time, which can be interpreted as another, although lesser, miracle.

Points to Ponder

- Whenever the disciples boarded their fishing vessel, Jesus more often than not performed a miracle, for instance, stilling a storm, catching a quantity of fish, and walking on water. But how did Jesus defy the laws of gravity and liquidity? The answer to this question

12-4-'15

can only be given by seeing Jesus as the Creator of the universe. Does not he who created both gravitational pull and bodies of water have control over that which he has made? Because of his divinity he has authority over the elements in nature.

- Jesus performed the miracle of walking on the Lake of Galilee to strengthen the disciples' faith and to assure them that they had nothing to fear. He identified himself with the words "I am,"* which in a sense is the very name of God. Note that Jesus uttered this selfsame identification in the Garden of Gethsemane with the result that the temple guards who came to arrest him fell to the ground. *1
- The disciples had to learn the lesson of Jesus's nearness in the midst of a storm. They spent their energy rowing a boat throughout the night. Although they made little progress, they saw Jesus's miraculous power over the laws of nature. For that reason they acknowledged and worshiped him as the Son of God.
- Paul wrote, "I am able to do everything through Christ who strengthens me." That means he could do all things in the presence of the Lord as long as he walked with assurance in Jesus's footsteps. Followers of Jesus encounter frequent storms in life, but as long as they know that he is standing next to them, they are safe. 2

*1 verify — not indicated in ESV footnotes.

2. I'm safe whether I realize it or not! As they were. PTL!

FEEDING THE FOUR THOUSAND

Matthew 15:29–39; Mark 8:1–10

Food for All

A wise teacher knows that repetition is the proven formula for learning well. To help students learn a lesson, the teacher must repeat it from time to time. Jesus was no exception to this rule. For example, the Gospels feature duplicate accounts of the Beatitudes, the Lord's Prayer, and the parable of the lost sheep.

The Gospel writers record the two miracles of feeding the five thousand and feeding the four thousand. Some people believe that this is one and the same miracle composed as two different reports. But the overwhelming evidence shows that there are two contrasting occasions, settings, locations, and methods. In the one, the people are with him a single day; in the other, they stay for three days. Even Jesus himself refers to these two incidents when he quizzes the disciples about the amounts of leftover food they had gathered. They answered that in the first instance there were twelve baskets full and in the next seven.

Crowds of people numbering into multiple thousands had come to Jesus. Among them were many sick and suffering: the blind, the crippled, and the mute. He healed them so that the blind were able to see, the lame walked, and the mute talked. Without a doubt there were many others who suffered loss of hearing, were demon possessed, or were handicapped in one way or another. Jesus healed them all with the result that they glorified the God of Israel.

The crowd stayed with Jesus for three days during which they had consumed all the food supplies they had brought with them. Jesus was moved with compassion; he realized it was time to act. If he sent the people home hungry, they might faint along the way.

Jesus's disciples asked where they could find sufficient food to feed so large a crowd. Their question was a simple matter of fact, for they already knew the answer. Of course they remembered what he had done earlier in feeding a multitude.

Same Miracle

Jesus asked the disciples how much bread they had with them, and they answered, "Seven cakes of bread and a few small fishes." This amount would be insufficient for the disciples, much less for a multitude. A crowd of four thousand men, not counting the women and children, needed to be fed. If Jesus could feed a crowd of five thousand with five cakes of bread and two fishes, he could just as easily feed four thousand with seven cakes and a few small fishes. If he could perform a miracle in the one case, he certainly could do it once more in the next.

This time there was no soft green grass on which the people could sit. There was only the hard ground with grass that had dried up. This indicates that the two accounts did not happen at the same time of year. Jesus told the people to sit down. He took the bread and in prayer offered words of thanks to God. Then he broke the flat bread cakes and continued giving them to the disciples who in turn distributed them to the people. Jesus did the same thing with the fishes, for which he gave thanks to God, and with the help of his men fed the crowds. Flat bread and fish made up a common meal for the people in the area of the Lake of Galilee.

At the moment Jesus broke the bread and fish, the miracle took place. No human being is able to explain how this feat was accomplished, for the act itself was a gift of God to his people through the hands of his Son. Everyone in the crowd ate until they were filled and thus received the energy to travel back to their homes.

Jesus instructed his disciples to gather the surplus so that everything would be neat and tidy. Nothing was wasted. The food they collected amounted to seven full hampers. These were sizable containers. If we consider that the apostle Paul was let down in a hamper over the wall of Damascus when he escaped in the middle of the night, we have somewhat of a mental picture of their capacity. There is no explanation of what was done with the extra food, but distribution to the poor is certainly an option.

Jesus once again proved to be the provider in both the spiritual and physical needs of the people. He dismissed the crowds while he and his disciples embarked and went to the other side of the lake. They sailed toward a town named Dalmanutha situated on the southwestern shore in the region of Magdala.

Points to Ponder

- The repetition of the miracle of bread and fishes stresses the fact that Jesus is the wonder-worker who cares for people in need. He beckons people to come to him, and when they respond and come to him, he blesses them with heavenly and earthly gifts and then gives them rest. Politicians call the crowds to come and listen to them. They promise many things, but they are unable to give them the gifts Jesus promises.

- Jesus shows his love to all people by giving them life's necessities. "The love of God is greater far than tongue or pen can ever tell." The crowd of four thousand, not counting women and children, was made up of Jews and Gentiles. The multitudes had traveled from far and near, which points to a mixed crowd. Throughout his ministry, Jesus helped believers and unbelievers alike. He praised Gentiles for their faith in him but rebuked unbelievers who had witnessed the miracles he performed in their midst but refused to believe. He compared them to the inhabitants of Sodom and Gomorrah, who would rise up against them on the judgment day.

- The disciples in this story were involved in the act of giving until everyone was supplied. All that Jesus supplied, the disciples gave to others, and in the end they gathered the leftovers. The lesson his people must learn is to give freely to those in need. Freely you have received, freely give. I have often challenged people to match God in giving gifts. Then I add the prediction that they will fail because God always grants many more blessings than we can imagine.

Paying the Temple Tax

Matthew 17:24–27

Question and Answer

Of all the four Gospel writers only Matthew, the former tax collector, tells the story of Jesus paying the temple tax—a tax that had to be paid annually for the upkeep of the religious services at the Jerusalem temple. It amounted to a half shekel, which was the equivalent of a worker's earnings for two days, and every Jewish male above the age of twenty had to pay this amount.

We do not know whether Jews disbursed this annual fee during their visits to the temple or paid the tax collector as he went through the countryside. Matthew tells us that tax collectors approached Peter and asked him whether his teacher paid the required temple tax. It became evident that both Jesus and Peter were approaching the due date and that this fee had to be levied before that specified day.

Even Jews permanently living abroad had to pay their dues and send the money to Jerusalem. While people disliked Roman taxation that made them subject to a foreign power, they had no objections to paying the temple tax because it had nothing to do with Rome. They knew that God had stipulated this tax to be paid for the continuation of Israel's religion.

The tax collectors may have thought that Jesus, as a teacher in Israel, should be among the first to obey God's laws and regulations. They approached Peter, the spokesman of the disciples, and asked about Jesus's neglect to pay the tax but said nothing about Peter being in arrears.

The reason Jesus had not paid on time may have been because of his work as a traveling teacher. Perhaps he and his disciples had been on a mission trip away from Capernaum. But Jesus could not be accused of willful neglect, for he would have been among the foremost to meet his obligations. It may have been that both he and Peter were short on cash at that moment. Otherwise there would have been no need to go fishing for a coin.

Another aspect of the miracle is that Jesus did not want to offend the tax collectors. Like any other Jewish citizen he paid his dues, and he also paid those of Peter, so that no further questions could be raised.

Jesus the King

The tax collectors asked Peter if Jesus paid the temple tax. Prompted by his sense of religious duty, Peter hastily replied, "Yes, he does." He assumed that Jesus would pay his annual share for the upkeep of the temple. Wanting to be sure, however, he went to the house where Jesus was and related the matter to him. But before he could speak, Jesus asked Peter a question. He inquired whether tolls and taxes are collected from kings and their sons or from others, that is, citizens and aliens living in their country.

Jesus's question touched on the theme of king and kingdom. In his Gospel, Matthew features this theme repeatedly.

For instance, the wise men came to Herod in Jerusalem and asked, "Where is the one born king of the Jews?" This means that Jesus, born into the royal family of David, came to rule as king. Indeed Scripture calls Jesus King of kings and Lord of lords. To consider him an earthly king of Israel in fact downgrades his matchless kingship. Jesus told Governor Pontius Pilate that he was a king in a kingdom not of this world but a king of a spiritual kingdom.

If Jesus is king in that spiritual kingdom, why then does he have to pay the annual temple tax? A king should be exempt from all financial obligations in his kingdom. And if the Jews in Jesus's day understood God to be king over Israel, then Jesus as his Son ought to be exempt.

Even though Jesus could exercise his right to kingship, he did not want to give offense, especially not by excusing himself as well as Peter from paying taxes. Jesus did not want to cause any trouble from the tax collectors and their superiors. They certainly would not have accepted his claim to kingship.

Hence Jesus told Peter to go to the Lake of Galilee and cast out his fishing line and hook a fish. He even revealed that the first fish he caught would have a shekel in its mouth, which was sufficient to pay the tax for both Jesus and Peter.

Peter, the fisherman, cast out his line and caught a fish. When he opened its mouth, he found a coin that met the need of the day.

Although this episode appears to be a simple illustration of paying taxes that are due, one can ask the question whether it is a miracle. It would seem more natural to say that Peter as a fisherman was fortunate to catch a fish with a shekel in its mouth.

However, Jesus was fully in control of the situation: the emphasis in this passage is not on Peter catching a fish but on Jesus' sovereignty over creation. He knew with divine knowledge that the fish had a coin in its mouth. This coin was sufficient to pay the temple tax for two people; it was enough for both Peter and Jesus. The point in this brief account is that Jesus is the miracle-worker. This miracle was one in which Jesus himself was a partial beneficiary, together with Peter. All the other miracles Jesus performed for the benefit of others.

Points to Ponder

There is more to this story of the coin in the mouth of the fish.

- First, both Jesus and his disciples could have claimed exemption from paying the temple tax on the basis of their full-time service as teachers in Israel. But this argument would have created untold trouble for everyone: tax collectors, arbitrators, Jesus, and his disciples.
- Next, the fish Peter caught was a sizable scavenger we know as a catfish. It had seen the shimmering flicker of a coin descending toward the bottom of the lake and had snapped it up. It had tried to swallow the coin lodging in its wide throat, but it was unable to get rid of it until Peter caught the fish. There was no way of finding the rightful owner of the shekel, so Peter could not be accused of theft for taking it.
- Also, before Peter was able to tell Jesus that his taxes were due, he learned that Jesus knew about the matter by the question Jesus asked him about royalty not having to pay dues and taxes.
- Last, the catch of fish was not merely a miracle that provided an evening meal for Jesus and Peter. It highlights Jesus's omniscience and power over creation, including a fish with a coin in its mouth.

THE CURSING OF A FIG TREE

Matthew 21:18–22; Mark 11:12–14, 20–24

Breakfast

Apparently Jesus and the disciples had left the home of Mary and Martha in the village of Bethany. He had not eaten breakfast and was on his way to Jerusalem. Walking along the road, he spotted one of the many fig trees in the area near Bethphage (which means "house of figs"), a suburb of the capital city. Jesus walked up to the tree and looked for some small, edible figs, which are unlike the larger figs that ripen in the summer months. These early figs emerge together with the leaves in the latter part of March and the beginning of April and are forerunners of the harvest in late summer.

Jesus looked for figs and found nothing but leaves; it was not the season of figs. In short, his was an exercise in futility, for even if Jesus had found fruit it would have had but little food value to sustain him during the morning hours.

The lesson Jesus taught by means of this incident pointed, however, not to his physical needs but to the spiritual life of the people. They lived a life that was as barren as the branches of the fig tree, leaves without fruit. These people wanted to make Jesus king and appoint him as their leader to set them free from Roman oppression. But their attempt to make Jesus an earthly king, instead of acknowledging him as their Messiah, would never set them free from the burden of sin and guilt.

The Curse

Jesus looked at the tree and pronounced a curse on it. He said, "May no one ever again eat fruit from you!" Did Jesus punish this tree for not bearing fruit when he looked for it at a time of year when figs were not ripe? Was Jesus frustrated because he needed nourishment and the fig tree failed to deliver?

The answer to both questions is *no*. Jesus merely used the fig tree and the curse as an object lesson for the disciples. As the fig tree showed foliage but not fruit, so the Jews showed external worship at the temple but not spiritual growth. The temple area had become a marketplace and a den of robbers. Here merchants sold sacrificial animals at high prices and money changers charged exorbitant rates for people who needed coinage stipulated by the temple guards. By means of cursing the fig tree and cleansing the temple, Jesus demonstrated symbolically that religious Israel failed to bear fruit and would face an eventual demise.

A day after Jesus cursed the fig tree, it showed signs of withering. The leaves were droopy and began to fall. Even a casual observer could see that the tree had been seriously affected by Jesus's curse. It would die within days and then be deadwood ready for the fire.

As the fulfiller of messianic promises, Jesus had come to his own society, but his own people did not accept him. To be sure, the religious authorities rejected him in spite of

- all his teaching,
- all his miracles, and
- all his compassion.

The crowds in Jerusalem showed appalling insincerity and deplorable fickleness. They welcomed him with a loud "Hosanna" on Palm Sunday but discarded him five days later by screaming, "Crucify him!"

When on the following day Peter called Jesus's attention to the withering fig tree, Jesus responded by telling him to have faith in God. But what precisely does that mean? Faith means clinging to God and never letting go of him. To illustrate, faith can be compared to two sheets of glass that lie horizontally on top of each other. They appear to be inseparable as if they are glued together because no air can get in between them. The way to separate them is to slide the one sheet off the other. There is nothing between the two sheets. But when by an external force one sheet slides, air enters and adhesion fails. So faith in God continues until doubt enters and eliminates faith.

Jesus declares that the one who has faith can tell a mountain to be lifted up and cast into the sea and it will happen. This should not be interpreted literally but rather symbolically. The person who has faith can figuratively move a mountain of difficulties and succeed. That person is an overcomer who has received power and ability from God to do unbelievable feats in the interest of God's church and kingdom.

The miracle of the withering fig tree is the only miracle Jesus did that had no immediate beneficial impact on the disciples. Yet this miracle had a redeeming effect when seven weeks later on the day of Pentecost these disciples preached the gospel and three thousand people were penitent, cut to the heart, and believed in Jesus. That was the beginning of a harvest that finally will come to an end when Christ returns.

44

Points to Ponder

- Five days after the cursing of the fig tree, God removed himself from the temple in Jerusalem. This happened when Jesus died on the cross on Good Friday afternoon and the curtain in the temple split from top to bottom, so that it no longer separated the Holy Place from the Holy of Holies. God departed from the inner sanctuary in the temple by splitting the curtain, leaving the sacred place to full view, and indicating that his divine presence had left. From that moment God made his dwelling in the hearts of believers. There he resides and makes his temple (1 Cor. 3:16; 6:19).

- The clergy of Jesus's day displayed an external appearance of their religion but failed to demonstrate internal faith. Owing to their lack of faith, they faced God's impending judgment. They denied the rule of God and claimed that they had no king but Caesar. Today's equivalent can be seen in the world's masses who reject God, his Word, and his laws. As a consequence, those who refuse to listen to God have no fellowship with him and walk in spiritual darkness. Apostasy means being cut off from God forever.

- On the judgment day two kinds of books will be opened. These books contain the records of the deeds that each person has committed and every word that has been spoken. One is the book of conscience, which accuses all who appear before the Judge. All are held accountable for their deeds and words that testify against them. The other book is the so-called Book of Life. Everyone whose name is recorded in that book is declared forgiven, acquitted, and innocent. These people comprise the harvest Christ reaps in that day.

The First Catch of Fish

Luke 5:1–11

Empty Nets

Jesus addressed multitudes without the aid of a public address system, yet everyone could hear him clearly word for word. He made use of the setting and put it to his advantage. For instance, when the multitude crowded him on the beach of the Lake of Galilee, he saw an empty fishing boat belonging to Simon Peter. Jesus asked him to push it a little away from shore. Jesus sat down, which was a customary posture for public speakers, and then he taught the crowd who were sitting and standing on the beach and hillside. He used the boat as his pulpit and the smooth level of the lake as his sounding board. The water surface deflected his voice and reached everyone in the audience.

When Jesus finished his teaching session and the crowd dispersed, he talked to Peter and Andrew, who with fellow fishermen were washing and mending the nets. Jesus observed that the men had come ashore with empty nets after being out on the water throughout the night. Midmorning Jesus told Peter and his men to go out onto the deep part of the lake, let down their nets, and catch fish. This instruction coming from Jesus, who had been a carpenter in Nazareth, was too much for Peter, who was a fisherman in Capernaum. Simon Peter knew when and how to fish, and midmorning was not the right time. He certainly was not ready to accept an order from a carpenter-turned-teacher and make a fool of himself.

Simon Peter told Jesus that he and his fellow fishermen had been working hard all night long and had come to shore without a single fish. Nonetheless, he had great respect for Jesus, who had given him the name "Peter" at an earlier meeting when John the Baptist was preaching along the River Jordan. So he changed his mind and agreed to go out onto the lake to let down the nets.

Miraculous Catch

No sooner had Peter and his fellow fishermen rowed the boat away from shore and lowered their nets into the deep than the men knew they were onto a fine catch of fish. They began to pull in the nets slowly and were surprised at the mass of fish they had caught. The volume of fish was so great that the nets began to tear and some fish escaped. Because extra help was needed, the men signaled the fishermen John and James on the beach to come with their boat to help garner the catch. When they arrived, the extraordinary number of fish filled both boats to overflowing. Indeed the weight of the fish was so heavy that the boats were at the point of sinking.

For the seasoned fishermen such an unusual catch of fish in the middle of the day was unbelievable. They had never seen anything like it. They had toiled all night long and had come to shore empty-handed, but when Jesus told them to cast their nets into the water, their catch was phenomenal.

47

They thought of the monetary value of the fish, which was most welcome. They knew that this catch would support their families into the foreseeable future. But now there was work to be done, for as soon as the boats were ashore the fish needed to be crated and sent to market.

Simon Peter was overcome with awe in the presence of Jesus, whom he acknowledged as the Holy One, and he saw himself as a sinful man. Jesus, the carpenter, had performed a miracle that astounded this experienced fisherman. Peter now fell at Jesus's feet and asked the Lord to depart from him. In the presence of someone with supernatural power, he considered himself sinful and unworthy. The closer he came to Jesus's holiness, the more he saw his own shamefulness because of sin. He now realized the predicament of Isaiah, who saw the Lord on his throne and said, "I am a man of unclean lips" (Isa. 6:5). In Peter's case the focus was squarely on Jesus's divinity and Peter's sinfulness.

Knowing where a shoal of fish might migrate and being able to make a catch is not miraculous at all. Fishermen have testified that at times schools of fish in the Lake of Galilee are so densely pressed together that the water surface is stirred by countless jumping fish. It produces the appearance of a heavy rain falling on the lake.

But when Jesus instructed Simon Peter to cast the nets into the water, he spoke with divine knowledge whereby the natural way of catching fish turned into a miracle. As he performed this wonder he demonstrated that because of his divinity he controlled the fish in the Lake of Galilee.

The Master's Call

Peter, Andrew, James, and John were awed by the incredible catch of fish. Earlier they had met Jesus at the River Jordan where John the Baptist was baptizing. Afterward they had returned to Galilee to support their families as fishermen. Now Jesus had come to surprise them beyond measure by performing a miracle in the context of their own trade.

Jesus addressed Peter and said, "Don't be afraid. From now on you will be fishing for people." With these words he enrolled not only Peter but also Andrew, James, and John in a class of students who would receive Jesus's daily instructions. Eventually they would graduate and go forth as his apostles. The miracle Jesus executed was to reveal his divinity to the disciples so they would become fully cognizant of their calling. Theirs was a holy calling that meant being devoted to their Lord, being willing to give up their occupation, and being absent from their families.

Jesus spoke in the context of fishermen. He did not say, "I will make you sowers of the Word of God." And he did not say, "I will make you shepherds of sheep." Farmers who sow seed can assume with relative certainty that they will harvest a crop sometime later in the season. They may not always have a bumper crop, but seldom do they face a complete crop failure. And shepherds can be sure that lambs will be born in springtime. Although there is the probability that they will lose one or two lambs, they are confident that nearly all of them will live and reach maturity. But when fishermen are out on the water, they are unable to predict with any degree of certainty whether they will return with fish. Hence, Jesus called his disciples to be fishers of people, that is, they would have to rely on God to perform the miracle of a catch.

The calling of these men to be disciples was instantaneous and urgent. Peter and his associates pulled their boats ashore onto the land. They took leave of their families and followed Jesus. Notice that these men did not know

- where they would sleep,
- what they would eat and drink, and
- where they would go.

49

In obedience to Jesus's call they left all and followed him. They knew that Jesus would pay attention to their loved ones by caring for them.

Points to Ponder

- The purpose of this miracle was for Jesus to catch, so to speak, the first disciples in his net. This meant that these fishermen would give up their trade to become full-time students of their teacher, Jesus. They would have to trust that he would provide for all their physical needs and that he would also care for their families while they were away. If Jesus showed them an abundance of fish to fill the needs of the disciples and their families, they could be sure that he would continue to furnish them with provisions day by day.
- These former fishermen would no longer be engaged in catching live fish that would soon be dead. Instead they would bring the good news of salvation to people devoid of spiritual life so that they might live and receive God's gift of eternal life. These fishermen would be given the task of proclaiming the Word of God. As they witnessed the phenomenal growth of the church, they would see the miracle of dead-in-sin people turning to Jesus and becoming fully alive in him.
- When the Lord calls us to do something for him, we should not only show obedience but also faith and trust in him. When he calls, he also supplies our physical and spiritual needs. He never fails us. Similarly we ought not to fail him either.

OBEDIENCE DEMONSTRATES TRUST

The Second Catch of Fish

John 21:1–14

First and Last

At the first catch of fish, Jesus publicly called men to become his disciples. By performing the miracle of garnering an abundance of fish, he taught them that their future work would consist of bringing people into his kingdom. By the middle of the first century they would stand amazed at the phenomenal growth of the church.

In a few decades after Pentecost, the church spread from Jerusalem to Samaria, Antioch in Syria, Asia Minor, Greece, parts of Africa, and Rome. From Rome the gospel went forth to the boundaries of the Roman Empire. According to evidence available from Scripture and the church fathers, Paul traveled as far as Spain (most likely as far as Portugal).

At the end of Jesus's ministry, when he was about to send forth his apostles, he once more performed the miracle of catching fish. He did this by providing breakfast for them on the beach of the Lake of Galilee. He also showed them,

51

as he reinstated the apostle Peter, that they would go forth to feed the flock and shepherd the sheep.

When Jesus first called fishermen to become his students, they had been fishing all night long but came to shore empty-handed. They witnessed Jesus's power over his creation when he told them to let down their net and as a result they caught an abundance of fish. He proved to be their Lord and Master, who called them to discipleship and taught them to be his ambassadors.

Near the end of Jesus's earthly life, he instructed his disciples to return to Galilee. In obedience to his words they went back and then briefly pursued their former occupation to put food on the table for their families. They placed their nets in a boat, launched onto the lake, spent the night out in the open, and tried to catch fish. But after a night of hard work, they were tired and dejected, ready to return to shore with an empty boat. Once more Jesus showed them his supernatural power when he asked them to let down their net. As a result, they caught an unexpected number of big fish.

Jesus Preparing Breakfast

Having returned to Capernaum, seven disciples went fishing. They were Simon Peter, Thomas (a twin), Nathanael, the two sons of Zebedee, and two unnamed disciples. In the context of their family needs, they used their waiting time productively. If they could bring in a load of fish, they would once again be able to sustain their wives and children.

Seven men went fishing in one vessel. Presumably the boat belonged to Peter, who had a proven record as an experienced fisherman. But all night long, their nets remained empty. When dawn broke and streaks of vapor hung over the lake, they could distinguish the shoreline, but objects on the beach were vague. They could see a man standing on the beach but were unable to identify him.

When they rowed the boat closer to shore, they heard a distinct voice coming from this person. He asked them, "Friends, you don't have any fish, do you?" He seemed to perceive that their boat was empty and their spirits dejected. Their voices proved this fact when they answered him with a subdued "no."

Then the stranger told them to cast their net into the water on the right side of the boat, which they did. To their amazement, they were unable to drag the net because of the multitude of big fish. Immediately John knew that the stranger on the beach was no one else but Jesus. He said to Peter, "It is the Lord."

Instantaneously both men saw the connection between this fish catch and the one of a few years earlier when Jesus had called them to be his disciples. Now at the end of Jesus's ministry he once more demonstrated his divine knowledge by having them catch an abundance of fish. In short, here was a repetition of the same miracle.

Simon Peter, true to his impetuous nature, threw on his outer garment, which he had removed, jumped into the lake, swam the short distance of approximately a hundred yards to shore, and met Jesus. The other men were not as hasty as Peter. They continued the task of hauling ashore the net filled with fish.

When the rest of the men landed and stepped out of the boat, they saw that Jesus had prepared breakfast. On a charcoal fire he was broiling a fish and there was a cake of bread. He asked them to bring some of the fish they had just caught. In so doing they participated in the miracle that had just occurred. In fact, the presence of a fire, the fish, and the bread may have been a miracle by itself.

In the meantime, Simon Peter went aboard the fishing vessel, loosened the top of the net, and helped the men haul the net ashore. The catch amounted to 153 large fish and, in spite of the weight, the net did not tear.

Jesus invited the disciples to have breakfast with him on the beach. Yet the mood of the disciples was restrained. They knew they were in the presence of the resurrected Christ, and yet none of those present dared to confirm it by asking him, "Who are you?" Jesus took the cakes of bread and the fish and gave them to the disciples. He made food sufficient for all of them. Jesus was the host, and they were his guests.

This breakfast on the Galilean beach symbolically portrays the great banquet in heaven. Jesus will be the host and his followers the guests. His words, "Come and eat," will sound once again at that time.

Let's get the right perspective on this incident. The focus of this miracle is not on the number of fish that were caught. The number 153 is not symbolic but points to John, who as an eyewitness records precisely what occurred. This is also reflected in the distance of a hundred yards from shore as well as casting the net on the right side of the boat. John was there and recalled all the details.

The point of this miracle is that it demonstrated to Peter and his fellow disciples Jesus's divine power and knowledge that would continue to accompany them in their apostolic ministry. Even today Jesus's presence is with everyone who trusts in his word, "I am with you till the end of time."

Peter Reinstated

When breakfast was over, Jesus singled out Peter from the company of the other disciples. On the last day of Jesus's earthly life, Simon Peter had disowned Jesus three times in a row. Now at the beach alongside the lake, Jesus asked him three times uninterruptedly whether he loved him. Each time Peter answered in the affirmative, and Jesus replied successively:

- "Feed my lambs."
- "Take care of my sheep."
- "Feed my sheep."

When Peter heard the same question, "Do you love me?" for the third time, he was visibly hurt. He answered Jesus in a subdued voice, "Lord, you know all things; you know that I love you."

Before Peter could be fully restored as Jesus's apostle, the Lord pressed home three times the concept of love in a question-and-answer form. The significance of three times is for the sake of emphasis.

Now reinstated with new and added responsibilities, Peter would serve Jesus as head of the apostles, leader and spokesman of the mother church in Jerusalem, defender of the faith, missionary to Jews in dispersion and to God-fearing Gentiles abroad, and author of two canonical Epistles. The church, whether in Jerusalem or abroad, regarded Peter as Jesus's most respected apostle (because Paul identified himself as one not fit to be called an apostle).

Points to Ponder

- This is the last miracle Jesus performed before he ascended to heaven. With it he concluded the series of miracles that accompanied his ministry. The apostles received God's spiritual gift to do miracles in support of their preaching. But with the passing of the apostles in the first century, their authority ceased.
- The New Testament teaches that only Jesus appointed the apostles. After spending a night in prayer, he named twelve men to be his disciples. When Judas committed suicide, the apostles cast lots to appoint a successor. But it was Jesus who controlled the lots and chose Matthias.

At the gates of Damascus, the Lord called Paul to be the apostle to the Gentiles. However, when James of Zebedee was beheaded, he called no one to take his place (Acts 12:2). And Paul refers to his apostleship as of "one abnormally born" (1 Cor. 15:8).

- The miracle of the first catch refers to the disciples as fishers of people; the miracle of the second catch focuses attention on their calling as shepherds of sheep. In the first incident Peter saw himself as a sinful man and in the second as a restored man who was instructed to care for God's people.

- As Jesus instructed the disciples to cast their net into the lake and catch fish, so he instructs his followers today to bring the gospel message to the people and have God perform the miracle of bringing them to repentance, faith, and salvation.

SICK MADE WELL

PETER'S MOTHER-IN-LAW

Matthew 8:14–17; Mark 1:29–31; Luke 4:38–39

All in the Family

As was his custom, Jesus faithfully attended worship services in local synagogues where he regularly taught the people from the pages of the Old Testament Scriptures. On one particular Sabbath morning, he preached in the synagogue of Capernaum, where he had made his home.

During that worship service while Jesus was preaching, a demon-possessed man cried out, "What do we have to do with you, Jesus of Nazareth? Have you come to destroy us? I know who you are, the Holy One of God." Jesus rebuked the evil spirit and said, "Be quiet and come out of him!" Shouting loudly, the demon left the man, who appeared unhurt even though the demon had thrown him to the floor. Everyone in the synagogue was amazed because Jesus not only presented new teaching but also demonstrated great authority in casting out demons.

Immediately after the worship service, Peter and his brother, Andrew, invited Jesus to accompany them to Peter's house. John and James, sons of Zebedee, came along too. The purpose for the invitation was to ask Jesus to heal Peter's mother-in-law, who lay sick in bed with a high fever. The disciples told Jesus about her condition and reasoned that if Jesus could restore the health of a demon-possessed man, he might be persuaded to heal the patient in Peter's house too.

Luke, identified as the beloved physician, wrote an interesting little detail in his Gospel, namely, Peter's mother-in-law had a *high* fever. This physician turned Gospel writer always had a penchant for correct medical reporting and constantly includes additional details:

- a man was *covered* with leprosy
- the withered *right* hand of a man
- a slave who was ill and *near death*

In addition, Luke reports that Jesus entered the bedroom of the sick lady, bent over her, touched her hand, and then rebuked the fever. Jesus showed tender loving care by his actions. Taking her by the hand, he helped her get up and demonstrated that she was completely healed.

As soon as Peter's mother-in-law got up, she wanted to express her gratitude to Jesus. She did this by preparing a delicious meal for Sabbath dinner and serving it to the men who had entered her home.

How did the miracle of healing this unnamed lady take place? The story relates that Jesus rebuked the fever, took her by the hand, and raised her up. The act of rebuking a fever indicates that some malady had entered her body. By performing this miracle in the privacy of a home, Jesus revealed himself as the Messiah.

Healer of Diseases

If we look at the healing of Peter's mother-in-law from a twenty-first-century perspective, we would be hard-pressed to call it a miracle. Many people today suffer from a high fever, and physicians know what to do with medicines that lower the body temperature and bring healing. Sometimes within a short interval a fever disappears and the patient is on the road to recovery. It would be reasonable to say that some of Jesus's miracles may lose their significance in light of modern-day medical progress.

Today's physicians, however, cannot claim to have the same power to heal the sick that Jesus demonstrated as reported by the biblical evangelists. Indeed, with all the available drugs and the latest medical equipment, doctors are unable to guarantee every sick person full restoration to buoyant health.

By contrast, Jesus healed the sick in his day by merely speaking a word from a distance away from the patient or by a simple touch. Jesus proved to be the Great Physician whose healing power was limitless. To illustrate, lepers, who because of their disease had lost parts of their hands, feet, and head, were healed instantaneously with all their body parts back in place. Jesus also opened the eyes of a man who had been born blind and restored a man's withered right hand.

Although Jesus does not renovate human bodies today as he did in the first century, his presence is as real today as it was in earlier days when he walked along the Lake of Galilee or the city streets of Jerusalem. In answer to the prayers offered by his people, Jesus heals the sick by guiding and directing the hands of physicians today. Medical authorities are often unable to explain the rapid recovery of a seriously ill patient, the remission of cancer that was expected to spread throughout a body, or the subsiding and disappearance of a chronic condition.

61

In Jesus's day, oil was used as a medicine; drugs and equipment are its modern equivalent. The healing power residing in the physical bodies of human beings is indeed amazing. Physicians stand in awe of this power when patients near death recover completely.

James, the half brother of Jesus, writes in his Epistle that sick people in the church should ask the elders of the church to come and pray over them in the name of Jesus. Jesus hears prayers offered in faith, makes the sick well, and raises them up. Without a doubt, Jesus's followers attest to the fact that he still performs miracles today in answer to prayer and because of childlike faith.

Points to Ponder

- As Jesus rebuked the winds and waves on the Lake of Galilee, so he rebuked the demon that had tortured a man who came to a worship service in the synagogue of Capernaum. After worshiping God, Jesus accompanied his disciples to Peter's house, and there he rebuked the fever that laid low Peter's mother-in-law. We do not think that Scripture instructs us to rebuke a physical ailment, but it does instruct us to bring our needs to God in prayer and to trust him for healing.

- David blesses God's holy name, praising the Almighty in his soul and everything within him. He puts his confidence in the Lord and tells his soul not to forget any of God's benefits, for the Lord, so he writes, forgives all our sins and heals all our diseases.

- This means that hidden sins must be confessed to purify the soul. When sin has been forgiven, the Lord sends healing and performs the miracle of restoring the body. Jesus makes the whole person well, body and soul. Nonetheless, the fact that Jesus brings healing

62

12/15

does not indicate all diseases are a direct result of a sinful act.

- Jesus made Peter's family life complete by healing his wife's mother. Through his miracles, he brought family members together again. Scripture teaches that we are the family of God.

Natural forces operate within the natural laws that Nature's God has put in place. He can direct them as He chooses.

A Man with a Withered Hand

Matthew 12:9–14; Mark 3:1–6; Luke 6:6–11

At Worship

The Gospels reveal that Jesus often healed people on the Sabbath, even during the morning worship service in a local synagogue. He made it known that the day of rest should be a day of joy and happiness for the worshipers. Jesus taught that God instituted the Sabbath for the benefit of the people and not the people for the Sabbath.

The clergymen of that day strictly observed God's Sabbath commandment and fulfilled it to the letter of the law. This meant that nothing could be done on the day of rest. But their strict obedience to the commandment had the effect of squelching the joy that the celebration of the Sabbath ought to generate. Instead, a stifling legalism ruled the day.

The clergymen wanted to test Jesus to see whether he would heal a person on the day of rest; they were watching him closely. They knew that on other occasions he had not observed the law of the Sabbath, according to their inter-pretation of this commandment.

On another Sabbath after the worship service, Jesus and his disciples had gone through the grain fields plucking heads of grain and rubbing them in their hands to have something to eat. The Pharisees had called on Jesus to rep-rimand his followers because picking heads of grain was the same as harvesting, and that was work, which was not allowed on the Sabbath.

Instead of reproving the disciples, Jesus had reminded the Pharisees of God's purpose for giving them a day of rest. God did not expect his people to become ritualistic in their observance of his law. He wanted them to joyfully celebrate that day and provide spiritual and material bene-fits to others.

On this Sabbath, the clergy slyly asked Jesus whether healing a person on the Sabbath was lawful. Their underlying motive was to level a charge against him for desecrating the day of rest. They did not seem to realize that if they brought an accusation against Jesus, this same charge could be turned against them for breaking the law to love one's neighbor. Their action comprised a grievous indictment not against Jesus but against themselves for the simple reason that heal-ing the sick on the Sabbath was not an evil act but one of love and compassion. Of course they also seemed to ignore the problem that if they were strict in obeying the Sabbath law, what would they do with the priests who worked harder on that day than on any other day of the week?

One of the worshipers this Sabbath morning was a man with a withered right hand. Perhaps the clergy had told the man to come to the worship service and petition Jesus to heal him. If Jesus fell into their trap, they could accuse him of desecrating the Sabbath and bring him to court. In their legalistic minds they reasoned that only a patient whose life was in danger should be healed on the Sabbath; a man with a withered hand could wait until the next day.

65

A Confrontation

Obsessed with bringing Jesus down, the Pharisees were unable to notice that he was fully aware of their evil intent. They asked him whether it was lawful to heal on the Sabbath. Jesus answered by giving them an example taken from daily life. He said, "If any of you has only one sheep and it falls into a pit on the Sabbath, will you not take hold of it and lift it out? By comparison, how much more valuable is a human being than a sheep!" He concluded positively, "Therefore, it is lawful to do something beneficial on the Sabbath."

Jesus placed before his adversaries the choice of doing good or evil and of saving or killing a human being. These were stark choices to which anyone would give the obvious answer of helping one's neighbor. However, the clergy remained silent, which could be interpreted that they had lost their argument and were defeated. Their silence also meant that they failed to show any sympathy for the man with the withered hand, whom they merely used for their evil purposes. They were in the synagogue not to worship God but to trap Jesus.

We are unable to know whether the man had always been afflicted with an emaciated right hand or if he had sustained an injury at work. His incapacity had severely disadvantaged him from doing ordinary manual labor. The Pharisees considered his shriveled right hand a blemish that restricted the man from fully participating anywhere in society and the synagogue. Instead of expressing sympathy and love, they looked down on him. Understandably, the man was ashamed of his inability to extend the right hand of fellowship to anyone meeting and greeting him. From the man's perspective, he would gladly be healed by Jesus so he could perform normal work and care for his family members.

Then Jesus looked around at his antagonists, became indignant, and grieved at their hardness of heart. They were supposed to be spiritual shepherds of the people. Instead they were interested in pulling Jesus down because he showed loving-kindness to the people. The Pharisees tried to accomplish their nefarious act by paying strict attention to the law of the Sabbath. But they failed to realize that God had given them the law to love him with heart, soul, and mind and to love their neighbors as themselves. By their actions they transgressed both parts of that law.

The man with the withered hand stood in the midst of the worshipers. Then he heard Jesus say, "Stretch out your hand." He did so in faith, and immediately his right hand was completely restored. Jesus did not touch the man's hand; he only asked the man to stretch it out for all to see. Performing an instant miracle, Jesus restored the man's hand so that he now could enjoy a normal life. There was no work involved for Jesus, who merely spoke, or for the man, who stretched out his hand.

We are not told what the reaction of the man was toward Jesus following the restoration. But we do know what the Pharisees thought about this healing miracle. They came together to plot how they might destroy Jesus. They were enraged and discussed among themselves what options they had in putting away Jesus.

With their warped minds the clergy considered Jesus's healing miracle a transgression of the law and the destruction of Jesus a deed that would merit God's favor. They were filled with envy because Jesus drew large crowds while they had to face a handful of people. He healed patients, which they were unable to do.

By executing the miracle of healing the man with a withered hand, Jesus did not do any physical labor and thus did not desecrate the Sabbath. He only spoke a word to the man who was healed. There was no breaking of the law, no cause to accuse Jesus, and no reason for dismay. There was joy and happiness for the man's restoration. But Jesus's opponents were blinded by sin and filled with rage. They were unable to see what he had accomplished.

Points to Ponder

- God gave human beings one day out of seven as a day of rest. He set the example by creating the world in six days and then resting on the seventh. He worked first and then rested on the last day of the week. Jesus rose from the grave on the first day of the week, which by the end of the first century was already called the Lord's Day. Christians rest on that day and work the rest of the week to show their gratitude to Jesus. They consider the day of rest a time for their physical, spiritual, and mental restoration. And they regard that day as God's gift to humankind.

- Sunday rest today signifies that Christians come together for worshiping God in spirit and truth. Since apostolic times, worship services are not confined to a certain location, such as Jerusalem, but are held anywhere and everywhere. And throughout the ages, so it has been.

- The Reformers of the sixteenth and seventeenth centuries stressed the sanctity of the Lord's Day. Indeed that day belongs to the Lord and should be filled to his praise and glory. That is, we should not spend the day in idleness or selfish pleasure but in activities that are a blessing to others. This is done through Christian fellowship, by teaching or preaching the Scriptures, and in visiting the elderly, the shut-ins, and the sick.

- We are part of an individualistic and mobile society in which it is hard to put down roots at times. Yet we as God's people must reach out to our neighbors and show them our love in Christ. Indeed, Scripture teaches that we must live in harmony with one another and overcome evil with good.

THE CENTURION'S SERVANT

Matthew 8:5–13; Luke 7:1–10

A Gentle Gentile

Numerous Jews came to Jesus with their requests for healing. Among them were two people: Jairus, who asked him to heal his daughter, and a royal official, who begged him to heal his son. But now a Gentile with the military status of a Roman centurion petitioned him to heal one of his servants. Jewish people felt free to approach Jesus, but Gentiles hesitated because Jews despised them and placed foreigners on the level of dogs. In addition, Jews had an aversion to military people, for they represented the hated Roman government, whose oppression they had to endure.

Nonetheless, New Testament writers put Roman centurions in a favorable light during the times of Jesus and Paul. Note these instances:

- At the cross a centurion calls Jesus the Son of God.
- Cornelius was a devout, God-fearing centurion.
- The centurion Julius was kind to Paul.

This proves that the Jews did not hate all military officers in the service of the Roman government. They honored and respected some of them because of their favorable disposition toward the people of Israel.

Luke tells us that a centurion residing in Capernaum loved God and attended the worship services in the local synagogue. This centurion had discovered that the Jewish religion proclaimed a message of purity, holiness, honesty, and justice. These qualities in life spoke volumes to him, for he too desired to live a virtuous life. Therefore he expressed a love for the Jewish people in that town. In return the Jews accepted him as a God fearer, namely, a Gentile who was not quite a convert but a friend nevertheless.

This Roman centurion believed in Israel's God and showed love to God's people. As a case in point, he was so concerned about the deteriorating health of one of his servants that he sent word to Jesus to heal the sick young man.

The centurion had heard Jesus preach in the synagogue of Capernaum and had seen him perform miracles. He fully accepted the preacher's messages and showed his faith by translating Jesus's words into deeds; he even donated a large sum of money to rebuild the Jews' house of worship. Because of his generosity and his attendance at the worship services, he was given a seat in the renovated synagogue.

By asking Jesus to heal his servant, the centurion demonstrated unusual love toward this young man whom he called "my boy." He expressed special endearment to him, for he cherished him as his own son. This servant was lying on his bed in terrible pain and giving every indication that his life was gradually slipping away. No physician had the ability to heal the boy's paralysis, yet the centurion firmly believed that Jesus could supernaturally restore him to vigorous health.

Jewish Intermediaries

The centurion made up part of the army serving Herod Antipas who was the Roman-appointed ruler of Galilee. By befriending the Jews and especially the leaders in Capernaum, the centurion had gained the respect of the Jewish population.

Although the centurion had come to know Jesus as a teacher of note who spoke with great authority and was a healer with superhuman power, he did not feel worthy to go directly to Jesus with his urgent request. The Jewish leaders were aware of the sick boy in the centurion's household, and they were ready to help the centurion when he asked them to serve as intermediaries between him and Jesus. Thus, with the help of Jesus's compatriots, the centurion dared to approach the Great Physician.

The Jewish leaders spoke highly of this Gentile who lived among them and had almost become a convert to their religion. They assumed the task of being the centurion's spokesmen to plead with Jesus to go and heal the paralyzed young man.

As a resident of Capernaum, Jesus must have known about this Roman military man who frequented the worship services and who had financed the reconstruction of the local synagogue. When the elders brought him the news of this stricken boy and the request for healing, Jesus readily consented to go to the home of the centurion.

We notice a chain reaction. The centurion acquainted the Jewish elders with his servant's condition; in turn the elders approached Jesus and acquainted him with the Roman centurion; as a result Jesus reacted favorably to their request.

For Jesus this meant entering the home of a Gentile, but Jewish purity regulations prevented him from doing so. The leaders apparently overlooked these laws in the interest of pleasing the centurion. In addition, Jesus made it known that his ministry was not limited to the people of his own nation but was open to everyone regardless of race, color, or nationality.

The Jewish leaders stated that Jesus should grant the centurion's request to heal the boy and said that he was worthy to be heard. But their remark did not square with the centurion's actions and words. The military officer did not come to meet Jesus personally because he made it known that he did not consider himself worthy to have Jesus come under his roof.

A Gentile's Faith

Friends of the centurion came to Jesus to relay a message from the centurion. They reported that he should not bother to come any further toward the house, for the centurion felt himself utterly undeserving to welcome Jesus. Through his messengers, the officer asked Jesus simply to speak a word of healing and that would be sufficient to heal the boy. He asked Jesus neither to see the patient nor to touch him. All he requested was that the Great Physician would speak words at a distance from the house and thus have the healing take place.

The words and the actions of the centurion speak volumes. Here is a picture of bedrock solid faith in action. The centurion knew that Jesus had authority to perform miracles; by comparison he saw his own authority as merely a faint glimmer. He said that he was a man under Roman authority and that he in turn had been given power to order the soldiers under him. He could command one of them to go and the soldier would go, another to come and he would come, and still another to do this or that and he would obey.

This officer did not deem himself worthy to have Jesus enter his abode, which was likely far more commodious than that of ordinary citizens. On the other hand, Jesus did not look at material riches. He discerned the man's faith, deemed him worthy, and granted his request.

In all humility the centurion said to Jesus: "Just speak the word and let my boy be healed." He was a man of faith fully aware of his unworthiness in the presence of Jesus, the Son of God. In short, the centurion did not consider Jesus to be an ordinary man but a man whom God had sent endowed with divine authority.

This military man acknowledged Jesus's prominence, majesty, royalty, and purity. His words not only reflected rank that in the armed forces was of utmost importance, they also indicated his submission to the highest power he had ever encountered.

No wonder Jesus commended the Gentile for a faith that overshadowed that of Jewish people in his day. Jesus said he had not found such great faith anywhere in Israel. He looked into the future and saw that Gentiles would turn to him in astounding numbers and would come from both the east and the west. They would sit at a banquet with the patriarchs Abraham, Isaac, and Jacob and all the prophets in the kingdom of heaven (Matt. 8:12). The unbelieving Jews, however, would be excluded from this heavenly feast; they would be cast out into outer darkness.

Jesus told the centurion through the intermediaries that his faith had been answered and had brought about the miracle of healing. The Great Physician had healed the boy from a distance without ever seeing him. When the friends of the centurion returned to the house, they found the boy in excellent health and back to his normal self.

Apparently when Jesus met Gentiles, he did not enter their homes but healed their sick from a distance by merely speaking a word to the caregivers. Another good example is the Syro-Phoenician woman near the city of Tyre, whose daughter was demon-possessed.

Points to Ponder

- Many times Jesus rebuked his disciples for their lack of faith. When they were afraid or doubted, he described them with the words "you of little faith." They had been taught the Scriptures and had Jesus as their daily instructor. To their shame, fear and distrust accompanied them.

- By contrast, a Roman centurion had not been instructed from his youth in the Scriptures and did not have the benefit of being Jesus's disciple. He displayed his full confidence in the one who commended him for having a faith greater than that of anyone in Israel. This Gentile was the forerunner of countless multitudes worldwide who would put their faith in Jesus.

- No psychologist can explain the miracle of healing that occurred at a distance from the patient. No faith healer can claim the same healing power Jesus displayed without seeing and touching the invalid.

- Jesus healed the sick not because of Jewish intermediaries but because of his own authority over sickness combined with a Gentile's unconditional faith in him.

- When we demonstrate complete trust in God's promises and acknowledge his all-embracing power, we experience definitive results because God never breaks his word. If we have faith as small as the tiniest of garden seeds, we are able symbolically to move mountains. In faith we know that he will make our paths straight.

THE NOBLEMAN'S SON

_____

John 4:46–54

A Jewish Official

Jesus returned to the town called Cana, where he had
turned water into wine at a wedding feast. While there, an
official of Jewish descent in the service of Herod Antipas
came to him with an urgent request. He had left behind a
son who was seriously ill and near death in his Capernaum
home. He had heard that Jesus had come from Samaria and
would eventually proceed to Capernaum.

The urgency of his son's illness forced this official to travel
to Cana, a distance of some twenty miles from his home.
We do not know whether he rode on the back of a donkey
or walked. He came to Cana in the course of the afternoon
and went directly to Jesus.

As a fellow Jew he could approach the Great Physician
and needed no help of an intermediary to convey his request. He knew from hearsay and other evidence that Jesus
indeed had supernatural power to heal his son. In fact, Jesus
had performed some extraordinary miracles in Capernaum.

That knowledge was sufficient for the officer. If Jesus had been the miracle-worker for others, he could do the same for his son.

The Jewish official wasted no time in addressing Jesus and begging him to come forthwith to Capernaum. But the Master seemed to hesitate, and instead of granting the officer's request, he took time to lecture the Galileans who surrounded him. He rebuked them for their faith that became evident only when they observed him doing miracles. Therefore their religion was nothing more than a charade. Their lack of genuine faith was embedded in curiosity and proved that they had no relationship with Jesus the Messiah. Their superficiality simply could not serve as an acceptable alternative to faith.

Although the official was standing next to Jesus and heard him address the Galileans, he had come to him driven by faith. That faith showed in his desire to have Jesus heal his son. His plea was that Jesus would come before his son died. When the Great Physician told him to go home because his son would live, his faith blossomed. He took Jesus at his word and immediately returned to Capernaum.

By instructing the official to return, Jesus assured him that his child would live. His command had the effect of increasing the man's faith. Because of the evening hour, the man could travel only partway and had to sleep in a nearby inn. But the next morning he continued on his homeward way. While he was still a distance from the house, his servants came to meet him with the joyful news that his son was alive and well.

The official had anticipated this news. Already before the servants were near him, he noticed their happy faces and heard their elated comments. He inquired at what time of day his son's health returned to normalcy. When he was told that it happened suddenly at seven o'clock in the evening of the day before, he knew that this was the exact time Jesus told him to return and that his son would be well.

Similarities

The similarities between the centurion and the official are unmistakable: Jesus performed both miracles from a distance—the one near the house of the centurion and the other some twenty miles from Capernaum. In the one case the patient was called a boy in the sense of "a son of the household," and in the other the sick person was a son. The two men were serving the same ruler, Herod Antipas, the one as a centurion and the other as an official. Both of them put their faith in Jesus and saw obvious results.

Yet it would not do to call these two incidents two renditions of the same event as it is sometimes depicted, which is clear from the differences that identify the two accounts. First, the one was a Gentile and the other a Jew. Next, Jesus elevated the faith of the centurion as the greatest, while that of the official increased in the course of time. Also, the Gentile was in Capernaum when he communicated with Jesus through intermediaries, but the official went to Cana and spoke directly to Jesus. And last, the illnesses were different: the one patient suffered paralysis, and the other had a fever.

Jesus rebuked the unbelieving Galileans who were interested in seeing him perform a miracle. They wanted to see a sign, but the official had not come to ask for a sign. He had come with the request to heal his son, who was near death in Capernaum, and by faith he believed that Jesus would hear his plea. That faith was answered with the simple directive to go home and the assurance that his son would live. When the official went home, he saw that Jesus had restored his son's health.

The joy in the official's home was exuberant. Everyone wanted to know exactly where Jesus was and what he said and did. They asked about the precise wording of the official's request, how Jesus had responded to him, and why he had addressed the crowd around him. The crowd wanted to see a miracle, and the miracle did indeed occur, but they never saw it happen.

The nobleman described Jesus as a man with divine power, the Great Physician, and the Messiah. He not only spoke of his faith in Jesus, but he also brought all the members of his household to faith in Christ. He became an evangelist for Jesus. Furthermore, his son was living proof of Jesus's power to heal the sick even from a distance.

Points to Ponder

- Christians do not need to see signs and wonders to believe in Jesus. What they must know and experience is Jesus's presence near them. They must acknowledge that he provides for them in all their daily needs. And those providential supplies are miracles in themselves, for they are answers to prayer. They must declare that the essence of faith consists of believing without seeing.
- Scripture clearly teaches that no one is able to please God without faith, that is, faith is an absolute requirement in approaching God. In fact, God regards as sin anything that does not have its origin in faith.
- Jesus healed sick people at a distance because of the caregivers' faith. He still answers prayers uttered by his people on behalf of loved ones, but they do not always receive an affirmative reply. Sometimes his answers are positive, at other times negative, and at still other times delayed.
- Jesus invites people of all races, colors, nationalities, countries, and languages to come and put their faith in him. No one is excluded, and everyone is regarded to be of equal importance in his presence. If Jesus regards all these people as his brothers and sisters, we should do likewise. In heaven all the ones who surround God's throne are without prejudice and are filled with love toward one another.

The Woman and Her Illness

Matthew 9:20–22; Mark 5:25–34; Luke 8:43–48

The Silent Sufferer

A woman living in Capernaum had suffered for twelve years from a loss of blood that weakened her physical body. She tried to hide the problem, but she was unable to cover up her pale complexion that told everyone she was ill. According to Levitical law, her loss of blood made her unclean. Thus, she was severely restricted in attending worship services in the local synagogue and could never contemplate traveling to the temple in Jerusalem. Whatever she touched was regarded as unclean, so she became an embarrassment to herself and the people around her. The Law of Moses stipulated that the bed she slept on, the chair she sat in, and the clothes she wore were all unclean. Any person who touched her or any of these items was also considered unclean.

This woman had tried every home remedy available to stop the flow of blood, but nothing seemed to help. The ailment, with its accompanying shame, had become part of her daily life. She was an outcast and lived the life of a solitary person.

The evangelist Mark tells us that time and again she had gone to medical doctors to find relief and a possible cure. But one after the other they had concluded that her ailment was a hopeless case and nothing could be done for her. Yet every time she went to a physician, she had to pay a fee. As the years went by her financial assets dwindled to the point that she was now poverty-stricken.

The woman suffered in silence. She knew that because there was no medical help for her, she would not live much longer. Her body was unable to cope with the continual drain on her blood supply. She would grow weaker as time went on until finally death claimed her life.

A person who is ill while surrounded by caregivers receives daily attention. But this woman suffering a loss of blood bore her affliction in silence because she had no one to help her. As an outcast through no fault of her own, she was devoid of both hope and help.

Help on the Way

Jesus had healed many people in Capernaum and elsewhere. As a consequence, innumerable people came with their sick and asked him to heal them. The woman suffering from a gradual loss of blood knew about Jesus's ability to make sick people well. She thought about going to this Galilean doctor who never refused to help those who were stricken by diseases.

When she came to the harbor front where she expected Jesus to be, she saw him arriving in a fishing boat while a crowd waited for him to disembark. Coming ashore, Jesus was surrounded by many people so that the woman immediately knew that it was impossible to approach him. She took a few moments to devise a plan for how to come near

Jesus. She firmly believed that if she could touch only the fringe of his coat as he passed by, she would be healed.

The woman put herself in a squatting position right along the road Jesus was taking into town. She was told by some people in the crowd to get out of the way or she would be hurt. But she waited patiently for Jesus to come near her as the crowd was forced to move around her. While she was sitting there, Jesus came near her, and a tassel at the bottom of his robe slipped over her hand when he walked past.

When the tassel touched her hand, she immediately felt an unseen power flow through her body restoring her health. Right away she knew that Jesus had healed her even though she had not addressed him verbally. She could feel renewed strength in her arms and legs. Although she could not see her face, she knew that her pale complexion had changed to rosy cheeks. Now she was a picture of health.

Suddenly Jesus stopped and asked the people, "Who touched me?" To them, this was a ridiculous question and caused his disciples to tell him that many in the crowd had touched him by their pushing and shoving. But the Galilean healer stood his ground and said that healing power had gone out from him. He scanned the crowd around him and then spotted the squatting woman nearby. According to the law she was unclean, and now since she had touched him, he too had become unclean.

The woman's embarrassment could not have been greater. In the sight of all the people Jesus singled her out, and she was unable to plead innocence. Trembling at Jesus's feet, she expected him to scold her. But when she looked up into his face, she knew that he would not reject her. His eyes reflected nothing but love and kindness.

Gathering up courage, the woman told Jesus about her physical condition, her desire to be healed, and her faith in him. She admitted that she had felt his healing power surging through her body and that at the same time the flow of blood had stopped. She knew she was healed.

Jesus looked at her and kindly addressed her with the word *daughter*, a term of endearment. Then he added, "Your faith has made you well. Depart in peace, and be free of your affliction." Jesus healed her physically and spiritually; he healed her whole person, for the phrase "made you well" refers to both body and soul.

The woman's faith may have been as small as a mustard seed, but it was sufficient to achieve the healing in her body. Her faith moved the mountains of loneliness, agony, worry, and poverty. By faith in Jesus she triumphed over all the odds that were against her.

Points to Ponder

- During Paul's ministry in Ephesus, sick people would touch one of his handkerchiefs or aprons that he had worn, and as a result they were healed. This does not mean that persons suffering from a malady should touch the clothes of a faith healer to experience healing. It is not the cloth but Jesus who heals the sick; it is not the robe but Jesus who restores the woman. There is a difference between cloth and confidence, fabric and faith.

- When something clean comes in contact with something unclean, for instance, when a white dress comes in contact with soot, the clean becomes unclean. This is not the case with Jesus, who is the source of purity and holiness. He turns that which is impure and imperfect into objects of holiness and perfection. He has the power to cleanse our sins that are red as scarlet and make them white as snow.

- Faith is the avenue through which the power of God flows freely to sinners who put their confidence in Christ. It is a conduit that delivers the blessing of healing from God the Father to his trusting children.

- We at times ask ourselves, "What would others think of me, if I ask Jesus to heal me?" Far too often we are hindered by fear of what relatives, friends, or acquaintances might say about our actions. We crave social approval and as a consequence fail to come to Jesus. Often he is the last one who is told about our problems, whereas he should have been the first one to know them. If I claim him as my friend, I ought to go to him right away and freely tell him my troubles. He is willing to listen and stands ready to help.

The Crippled Woman

Luke 13:10–17

A Spinal Curvature

For eighteen long years a woman had been unable to straighten her back. Her ailment was probably something we know as a deformity of the vertebrae that had gradually fused. In a relatively short period her spine was completely bent double with the result that she always had to look down as she walked. She was unsteady on her feet and had to use a cane to give her a measure of stability.

The woman's physical condition brought about an imbalance of her nervous system so that both body and mind were unwell. The woman was in a pitiable condition that no physician was able to heal.

Jesus accurately analyzed her spiritual condition when he said that Satan had bound her for eighteen years. This means not that she was a demoniac but rather that her crippled condition was caused by the devil. That evil spirit was the real cause of her deplorable state.

Nonetheless, the woman was free to come to the Sabbath worship services to hear the Word of God explained by the local preacher. One particular Sabbath she had made her way to the synagogue and there learned that the leader of the synagogue had invited the prophet Jesus of Nazareth to preach. She had heard many stories about this prophet and especially the report about his healing power. With anticipation she sat down and waited for the service to begin.

The woman pondered the thought whether Jesus would take note of her condition and perhaps grant healing. Because she was a woman, she did not have the freedom to approach Jesus as a man could. Indeed, due to her condition she had trouble focusing attention on Jesus during the service.

An Unexpected Response

When Jesus finished his teaching lesson, he looked at the crippled woman and said, "Woman, you are released from your infirmity." The word *woman* was culturally acceptable in those days much the same as we would politely address a lady with the term *madam*.

Jesus placed both hands on her shoulders, and then a powerful surge entered and flowed through her body. Immediately she noticed that she was healed physically and mentally. She could sit up straight, and the pain that had been her constant companion was gone. She was set free from her bondage in both body and mind. Satan had lost his grip on her, for now she could stand up straight and did not need her cane anymore.

What a joy and relief! The woman could not restrain herself and in a loud voice praised God with words of thanks. She wanted everyone to hear that a miracle had taken place. Although she had not petitioned Jesus to heal her, yet her devotion to God was evident in her faithful attendance at the worship services. She had patiently waited for her God who suddenly through Jesus had healed her.

The woman expected everyone in the synagogue to rejoice with her. And this is exactly what happened. All the worshipers were expressing their joy with her. They all glorified God because a miracle had occurred in their midst.

However, the leader of the synagogue was not pleased at all with what Jesus had done. He did not address Jesus directly but spoke to the congregation. He said, "There are six days in which work must be done. On those days come and be healed, but not on the Sabbath day." The only work, if it can be called work, Jesus had done was to put his hands on the shoulders of the woman and address her with the words, "Woman, you are released from your infirmity."

The leader acknowledged that Jesus was a healer of diseases, but he objected to him doing it on the Sabbath. He had no objection to healing but, according to him, it must not be done on the day of rest. He was a strict legalist who saw Jesus as a lawbreaker whose actions dishonored the leader of the synagogue. He felt it was his duty to rebuke the guest preacher for stepping over the line in regard to Sabbath observance. He knew he had to uphold the legal system of their culture and thus had to speak.

Jesus reacted not to the jubilant congregation but to the pettiness of the synagogue leader and his associates. He called them hypocrites and made it clear that their view of keeping the Sabbath was not the will of God. To explain what he meant he used an illustration from everyday life. Anyone owning an ox or a donkey would take the animal out of its stall on the Sabbath and lead it to the watering trough so it could drink. Would the synagogue leader call this work? He would respond, "Of course not, because that is necessary."

Jesus's argument goes from the lesser to the greater. If it is necessary to take care of animals on the day of rest, is it not also necessary to take care of God's people on that day?

The answer is obvious because his people are prized much higher than the rest of God's creation.

If animals must be released from their stalls on the Sabbath, must not human beings be released from their chains on that same day? If Satan bound this woman with a severe infirmity for eighteen years, would it not be necessary for Jesus to release her from Satan's chains without delay? Satan had bound this woman all these years in his kingdom of darkness, but Jesus called her a daughter of Abraham and released her into his kingdom of light.

The ruler of the synagogue and his associates had tried to accuse Jesus of breaking the law. But Jesus's words exposed their hypocrisy, and they were put to shame in the presence of the worshipers.

The people at the service rejoiced because of the glorious things that Jesus did and continued to do. It was not only the healing of the crippled woman but many other wonderful healings as well. Jesus revealed his power to destroy Satan's impediments placed upon the people that kept them in bondage. He saw the destructive effect of Satan's rule on this earth and opposed him by restoring the sufferers to robust health. Not Satan but Jesus has the last word, because he is the Victor and Satan the vanquished.

Points to Ponder

- Jesus did his work of teaching in the synagogue and healing on the Sabbath out of love for his fellow human beings. He showed that the law of love transcends the law of the Sabbath. Yet the one does not cancel the other, for both remain intact. The law of love is spelled out in the summary of the Ten Commandments and therefore always supersedes them in every situation.
- The love we owe our neighbor ought not to set aside the command to observe the day of rest. Both can and

often must be observed on that same day. Jesus used his powers of both teaching the Scriptures and healing the sick for the benefit of the people. He teaches us the lesson to honor God's commandments in such a manner that we demonstrate our love for God by loving our neighbors as ourselves.

- It appears that Jesus repeatedly healed people on the Sabbath and invariably was rebuked by the Pharisees and teachers of the law. His objective was to remind the people that the Sabbath is a day of rest and gladness, not a day of gloom and doom. The apostle Paul writes this rule of life: "Rejoice and be exceedingly glad, and again I say, rejoice."

- Jesus calls the woman a daughter of Abraham, not that she becomes one but rather she is one. She belongs to the covenant that God made with Abraham and his offspring. This means that claiming these covenant promises she is a recipient of God's faithfulness and grace. We too are in that same covenant through the mediatorial work of Jesus our Lord. All the rights and privileges God gave Abraham are ours through Christ's atoning work on the cross.

A Man with Dropsy

Luke 14:1–4

A Dinner Guest

Jesus was the guest preacher in many synagogues, especially in Galilee, but also in Judea. After a Sabbath morning worship service, the guest preacher usually was invited by a distinguished leader in the community to have dinner with him. Most often this leader happened to be a Pharisee who not only knew the Scriptures but also was a meticulous observer of the law and particularly of the commandment to keep the Sabbath day holy.

Depending on the weather, the host would serve the Sabbath meal outside in his courtyard rather than in a crowded room inside. With extra tables to accommodate a number of guests, among them learned teachers and Pharisees, the meal could be a festive occasion because it was always well prepared. The topic of conversation, however, would set the tone of the gathering, which might become unpleasant if the host and guests disagreed among themselves.

The host had listened to Jesus's exposition in the synagogue and perhaps was not happy with the sermon. Could it be for this very reason that after the service the host had invited to dinner a man who was suffering from dropsy? This is a disease that causes extra water to collect in the areas of the neck, arms, and legs as well as other parts of the body. Medical knowledge was underdeveloped, and physicians in that day were unable to treat patients who were suffering from this disease. In spite of the water retention in his body, the patient was able to attend many of the activities in the village where he lived.

We assume that the host had invited the man to test Jesus on his attitude toward Sabbath observance. He wanted the teacher to deviate from accepted norms so that he and the guests could accuse Jesus of breaking the law. During the meal they watched Jesus carefully to see what he would do with respect to the man with dropsy. Would Jesus heal the man on the Sabbath and thus desecrate the day of rest? The host set the tone at mealtime, and consequently the conversation was subdued. People felt that the pervading atmosphere was not right and that something was bound to happen.

Although Jesus was the honored guest, the host and guests failed to show him due respect. Instead of conducting an animated and pleasant conversation, they were quietly watching Jesus as if he were ignorant of their motives.

Wherever he was, Jesus preached love for God and love for one's neighbor. When there was an opportunity to put his words into deeds, he would show love in action. Of course he was fully aware of the Pharisees' intentions, but he wanted to teach them that love for one's neighbor surpasses the law of Sabbath observance.

Jesus asked the learned theologians and the Pharisees whether it was lawful to heal on the Sabbath. Having posed the question, he faced absolute silence. The host and his guests realized that they had met their match, for Jesus had cornered them with a simple question of doing something good on the day of rest.

The Aftermath

Jesus was in full control of the situation. It was not the host or his guests who asked the question whether it was lawful to heal on the Sabbath. Jesus did. They were defeated, but they were poor losers. Their hardened hearts made them resist Jesus and show hostility toward him, while he put the matter in the context of doing a good deed on the Sabbath out of love for a fellow human being.

Caring deeply for the suffering man, Jesus put his hand on him and restored his body. This was a miracle. The man's kidneys had worked poorly, but now they functioned normally, and the extra water in his body suddenly disappeared. The man's appearance changed completely. Indeed the people could not help but see the radical transformation in him. The man was filled with joy and happiness and left after speaking a word of thanks to Jesus.

Jesus continued to address the host and learned guests at the dinner table. He used an example that illustrated a not unusual experience of daily life. He asked, "Who of you, if your son or your ox falls into a well, will not pull him out immediately on the Sabbath day?" The answer to this question was obvious, for one's love for a son or care for an animal would call for immediate action. Jesus paralleled the possible drowning of a son or ox in a well with that of the man who had excess fluid in his body.

Jesus's winsome attitude toward the people at the meal taught them how and when to love one's neighbor. With a graphic example taken from daily life, he was able to instill in them the basic principles of God's Word.

Points to Ponder

• The invitation the Pharisee extended to Jesus to have dinner with him after the morning worship service was in itself commendable. Jesus teaches that when you invite guests to your home, you should not just invite friends and acquaintances who will repay you by inviting you back. But you should ask the poor and people with physical handicaps to come to your table, for they will be unable to pay you back. You will receive your reward on the day of resurrection.

• The Gospels indicate that Jesus often performed miracles on the Sabbath. Indeed, there are a total of seven incidents: the man at the Pool of Bethesda, the man born blind, a demon-possessed man in Capernaum, Peter's mother-in-law, the man with the withered hand, the man suffering of dropsy, and the crippled woman. By means of all these miracles Jesus taught the people to celebrate the Sabbath with joy and happiness. The Sabbath was meant for a time of spiritual revival with God's people at worship.

• God asks us to obey his law, and if we do so, we thrive and live in harmony with him and with our fellow humans. If we keep the law for the sake of the law without love, we no longer serve God and are transgressing the law we are told to keep. By contrast, if we joyfully celebrate the day of rest to honor him, we receive benefits for ourselves and our neighbors. If we show love toward our fellow citizens, we are walking in the footsteps of Jesus.

• God tells his people, "I will forgive their wickedness and will remember their sins no more" (Jer. 31:34). As far as the east is from the west, so far has he removed our iniquities from us (Ps. 103:12). Note that Scripture does not use the wording "the north from the south," for that is a distance that can be measured. Although we know the circumference at the equator, we are unable to tell where east begins and west ends. God's forgiving love knows no bounds.

- Jesus sets the example for us to follow and walk in his footsteps. That means that we must walk behind him and not in front of him. Far too often when we want to do something for the Lord, we fail to consult him and go our own way. Afterward we tell him what we have done and then realize that we failed to gain his approval. Then to our shame we understand that we have been putting the proverbial cart before the horse. We should ask Jesus what he wants us to do for him and then in loving obedience do the task to the best of our ability.

MALCHUS

Luke 22:49–51; John 18:10–11

The High Priest's Servant

One of the servants of Caiaphas the high priest was called Malchus. He was not a member of the temple guard but rather a faithful servant in the house of his master.

Malchus had heard about Jesus and perhaps had listened to him in the temple area where the prophet from Nazareth occasionally taught. But late one evening the high priest had been in a prolonged meeting with the Pharisees. Later he gave orders to his officers and the Pharisees to arrest Jesus. He indicated that Malchus also should accompany the soldiers and police officers. He made it known that one of Jesus's disciples would lead the way toward the Garden of Gethsemane where the teacher supposedly was hiding under cover of darkness.

These police officers known as the temple guard often exhibited aggressive behavior that led to violence. Malchus was especially eager to capture Jesus. As the soldiers and the officers carried weapons, he took along a short sword to administer a blow if need be. Others also were well armed with clubs and swords. They knew that Jesus would be surrounded by his devoted followers, who undoubtedly were prepared to defend their Master and put up fierce resistance.

Guided by Judas, who was one of Jesus's disciples, the entourage set out from the house of the high priest and went across the Kidron Valley toward the Garden of Gethsemane. They carried lanterns and torches to light the way. When they arrived at the garden, they saw Jesus and his men among the olive trees. Judas had told the band that he would give them a sign to point out Jesus. He would walk up to Jesus and kiss him. Then they could capture him, tie him up, and take him to the high priest.

Judas walked right up to Jesus and kissed him on the cheek. All along Jesus knew that Judas would betray him, but the brazen act of kissing him as a prelude to capturing his teacher was downright treachery. Jesus said to him, "Friend, do what you came for. Do you betray the Son of Man with a kiss?"

Jesus asked the band of soldiers and officers, "Who is it you are looking for?" They answered, "Jesus of Nazareth." And he replied, "I am the one." Judas the traitor stood there with them. But as soon as Jesus had uttered the words *I am*, they all lurched backward and fell to the ground. Here his divine majesty was obvious, showing that not the soldiers but Jesus was fully in control of the situation. He was not filled with fear but showed his royalty as king. In the presence of Jesus, the group of officers, soldiers, and servants, including Malchus, fell to the ground.

After they scrambled to their feet, Jesus asked them once more whom they sought, and they gave the same answer: "Jesus of Nazareth." He said, "I told you that I am he. If then you seek me, let these men go." Without a doubt, Jesus was true to his word that not one would be lost of those the Father had given him, except the son of perdition, Judas.

Peter's Reaction

Before the disciples left for Gethsemane, Jesus had told his followers to take along a purse and a bag and to buy a sword if they did not have one. The disciples came well prepared and made it known that they were in possession of two swords. Jesus told them that two swords were enough. Peter as the spokesman had one of them.

Perhaps Malchus was wielding his short sword in preparation for capturing Jesus. His action was a sufficient signal for Peter, with sword in hand, to defend his Master. He swung his weapon toward Malchus and cut off the man's right ear. In response to this action, Jesus commanded Peter to put his sword away, for he knew that it was the Father's will that he had to suffer. He said to Peter, "No more of this violence." Then he picked up Malchus's ear and put it back in place, performing a healing miracle right on the spot.

For Malchus it would have been a lifelong blemish if Jesus had not reattached the ear. Even in the hour of his arrest, Jesus showed mercy to one of his captors. He did not want to provoke any violence on his behalf, and thus he reminded Peter that those who live by the sword perish by it. In regard to defending him, he said he could call his Father to send twelve legions of angels to protect him. And he added, the Scriptures had to be fulfilled that he should suffer.

The sequel to this incident is that Peter with another disciple, possibly John, followed the captured Jesus all the way to the house of the high priest where the trial took place. He did not enter the house but stayed in the courtyard, where the soldiers had lit a fire to keep themselves warm because it was cold. Peter mingled with the people until a girl asked him whether he was one of Jesus's disciples, but he said that he was not.

As Peter was warming himself, the people standing next to him asked, "You aren't one of his disciples, are you?" Peter said that he was not one of Jesus's followers. Then a person who was a relative of Malchus, whose right ear Peter had cut off, recognized Peter and challenged him by asking, "Did I not see you with Jesus in the Garden of Gethsemane?" Others were saying that his speech identified him as a Galilean. Now Peter was caught because of the evidence. He should have owned up and admitted that he belonged to Jesus. But sadly Peter renounced his Master a third time by calling down curses upon himself.

At that moment the rooster crowed and Peter realized he had denied Jesus three times in succession. He went outside the courtyard and wept bitterly.

Points to Ponder

- Judas betrayed Jesus while Peter denied him. Both went outside, but the one wept bitterly and the other hanged himself. Although both regretted their actions, there was a vast difference between these two disciples of Jesus. Judas was filled with remorse that is self-pity; his feelings of remorse stayed with him and had no outlet. He returned the blood money to the chief priests and elders, but they showed him no mercy. They told him that remorse was his own responsibility. Mercy flows forth from God but never from the devil. Judas had to solve his own problems.

- Peter repented and wept bitterly. He returned to the disciples and eventually to Jesus, who forgave him and reinstated him as an apostle. After Peter was restored, he served Jesus as head of the apostles and of the Jerusalem church. Judas had nowhere else to go, and so he committed suicide. That was the worst thing he could do, because upon death he faced the Judge who condemned him.

- True repentance means that you reach out to the person whom you have offended and ask him or her to forgive

97

you. Forgiveness implies not only that the record is wiped clean but also that the sinful deed is forgotten and will never be mentioned again. True repentance means that the one who forgives a sinner will never mention his or her evil deed again. The record is cleared, and relations are fully restored to what they were before the incident.

EARS TO HEAR

A Man Blind and Mute

Matthew 12:22–32; Luke 11:14–26

Impaired and Healed

Imagine a person who is unable to see and speak and only has the senses of hearing, taste, touch, and smell. The world around him has no meaning at all because of a lack of verbal and visual communication. Then imagine that he is possessed by an evil spirit that affects the mind of this severely handicapped person. This double impairment plus being demon-possessed is enough to declare his life meaningless. Think of the loneliness such a person must experience in addition to the torture of a mind completely controlled by a demon.

Medical experts today would readily admit their inability to examine a person with these impairments, let alone try to find a cure for him. Various parts of the man's body, for instance the optical nerve, were never developed. In the absence of functional parts relating to speech and sight, the man could not expect any medical help at all from fellow human beings. He was a loner, and because of an erratic mind he was shunned by everyone, including some of his own relatives.

Immediate family members brought the impaired man to Jesus, who cast out the demon and healed him so that he could both talk and see. This indeed was a miracle of the highest order, which had never been witnessed in Israel.

The Gospel writers say nothing about the man's faith to be healed or a request for healing. But it is not difficult to understand that the impaired man could not make his wishes known to Jesus. The Gospels are silent about the reaction of the man after he was healed.

Amazement and Questions

Crowds of people were present when Jesus healed this hapless man. When they witnessed Jesus performing the miracle, their amazement knew no limits. They were saying repeatedly that they had never witnessed anything like this in Israel. Because of the Scriptures they were knowledge-able about their past, but they could not think of anything similar in Israel's history.

If Israel's past was silent about a healing miracle such as this one, they asked themselves whether the promised Messiah had come and was now performing miracles in their midst. From the prophetic books, they had learned that in the messianic age miracles and wonders would occur. They inquired whether it was possible that the Son of David, the Messiah, was standing among them. They had no certainty and no way of knowing, but they could ask the Pharisees and the teachers of the Law what the Scriptures said about this matter. They expected that these learned men should be able to answer their question. Certainly, these educated people could recite from memory large portions of the Old Testament.

The prophecy of Isaiah, written more than seven hundred years before the coming of Jesus, predicted in various places that the messianic age would usher in miracles, among which was giving sight to the blind. In the entire history of the Old Testament era, no blind person had ever experienced restoration of sight, but in the messianic age this would happen.

Now that Jesus had given sight and speech to a demon-possessed man and had cast out an evil spirit, the crowds were astounded. They swarmed around the man who now addressed them in coherent words and looked them straight in the eye. They asked if the prophecies in the Book of Isaiah were being fulfilled right in their midst. Could Jesus be the Messiah promised in the Scriptures?

To whom could the people turn but to the Pharisees, the teachers of the Law, and the scribes who had witnessed the miracle? These leaders had a thorough knowledge of the Scriptures and could tell the people exactly whether prophecies were being fulfilled that very moment. Actually, they had expected these learned men to shout at the top of their voices that Jesus was the long-expected Messiah. These scholars should be the first to announce the good news.

Furthermore, this was not the first miracle Jesus had performed. He had cleansed lepers, made the lame walk, opened the ears of the deaf, given sight to the blind, raised the dead, and healed the sick. And people everywhere were telling stories about the miracle-worker called Jesus. They were living witnesses to his divine power to perform wonders.

Although the people lacked factual knowledge, they asked a question to gain complete certainty. They cautiously framed their doubt in the form of a question that expected a negative response: "This one is not the Son of David, is he?" They wanted the clergy of that day to give them the assurance that the Messiah indeed was among them and tell them: "Yes, he certainly is!" Theirs was not a matter of reluctance to believe the obvious; all they needed was a forthright declaration from their religious teachers.

An Astonishing Denial

The learned scholars refused to answer in the affirmative the question of whether Jesus was the Son of David, that is, the Messiah. Even though they witnessed this astonishing miracle, the men schooled in the Scriptures refused to accept Jesus as the Messiah. They rudely addressed the crowd and told them that this fellow could only cast out demons with the power of the prince of demons, namely, by Beelzebub—another name for Satan. They refused to call Jesus by name but referred to him contemptuously as "this fellow." They wanted the people to believe that Jesus was in the employ of Satan.

The religious leaders saw their influence threatened by Jesus, who drew large crowds of people. The evidence was too strong and the testimony too powerful, therefore Jesus's opponents tried to discredit Jesus by saying that he cast out evil spirits by the power of the prince of demons. They did not say anything about Jesus fulfilling the messianic promises of giving sight to the blind and hearing to the deaf. They thought that in spite of the evidence the people might believe the lie. They said that Jesus had allied himself with the powers of the evil one, namely, the forces of iniquity.

Jesus then addressed the leaders and the people with words of common sense. He pointed out the ridiculous and inconsistent logic of his adversaries by saying that a divided kingdom comes to ruin and a divided household cannot last. He said that if Satan is involved in casting out Satan, he is ruined and his kingdom becomes void.

Jesus then turned to the clergy and asked them by whose power their people were casting out demons if, as they said, he was casting them out with the power of Satan. He told them that their exorcists would pass judgment on this matter. He said, "I cast out demons by the Spirit of God because the kingdom of God has come upon you." The people should realize that with these miracles God was at work establishing his spiritual kingdom on this earth. At the same time God through Jesus was robbing Satan of his followers by claiming them for Christ.

But Jesus had more to say to the Pharisees, teachers of the Law, and scribes. He told them in no uncertain terms that they had sinned grievously against God to such a degree they would never be forgiven. He informed them that blasphemy against the Son of Man, namely, Jesus, would be forgiven, but blasphemy against the Holy Spirit would forever be held against them and never be pardoned.

Those who knew and taught the Scriptures had blasphemed the Spirit of God by calling Jesus a servant of Satan when all the evidence of his teaching and works showed that he was the Messiah. They now faced an angry God who condemned them forever. In short, Jesus revealed to them that on judgment day they would face everlasting separation from the living God.

Points to Ponder

- Is it possible for a sincere Christian to sin against the Holy Spirit and be lost forever? Some Christians worry about having committed the unforgivable sin. But the Scriptures teach that to those who repent of their sins, God extends his grace and mercy and wipes the record clean. No matter how grievously they have transgressed his commandments, God forgives them. The good news is that Jesus has come to save sinners and welcomes all who repent and ask for remission of sins.

- The Scriptures clearly speak about the sin against the Holy Spirit that cannot be forgiven. The writer of the Epistle to the Hebrews notes that if we purposely keep on sinning after we have received the knowledge of salvation, then Christ's sacrifice on the cross has no meaning for us. Then we can expect God's judgment that rages like fire and consumes his enemies. Anyone who tramples underfoot the Son of God, who indicates that Jesus' shed blood is of no value, and who insults the person of the Holy Spirit, faces God's wrath. It is frightful indeed to fall into his hands.

A DEAF AND MUTE MAN

Mark 7:31–37

The Decapolis Region

To the south and the east of the Lake of Galilee was an area known as the Decapolis. Translated this name means "ten cities." Loosely connected in a confederation of ten Gentile cities, they were situated along trade routes leading from Damascus to cities in Arabia. The Decapolis flourished, and in Jesus's day it served as a buffer zone against marauders from the east for the Jewish areas situated to the west.

Jesus had visited Gadara in the western part of the Decapolis when he cast out multiple demons from a man called Legion. When the man set free from demons wanted to accompany him, Jesus told him to acquaint the local people with the news that God had changed his life. As a converted Gentile, he could minister effectively to his compatriots in the Decapolis and tell them the story of Jesus the miracle-worker from the land of Israel.

When Jesus returned from his journey to Tyre and Sidon in Phoenicia, he went around the eastern side of the Lake of Galilee into the Decapolis. As he was passing by, he healed numerous people who were lame, blind, crippled, and deaf. The people in that area praised the God of Israel and considered Jesus the miracle-worker sent by God. As a consequence, large crowds of Gentiles followed him.

Among those afflicted people was a man who was deaf and had a speech impediment. Friends brought him to Jesus and asked him to put his hands on him so he would be healed.

Notice that Jesus employed different methods to accomplish his healing ministry. At times a single spoken word of Jesus was sufficient to restore someone's health even at a distance. At other times, he spat on the ground, made mud with his saliva, and smeared it on the eyes of a man born blind. At still another occasion, Jesus healed a blind man in two stages: first by spitting on his eyes and then following it up by touching his eyeballs. All these methods brought healing to the afflicted.

Severely Restricted

Being deaf and hardly able to talk clearly is a handicap that is even worse than being blind. A blind person is able to communicate and hear all the sounds, but someone who is unable to hear and speak clearly lives in complete isolation.

This deaf man lived in his own restricted world. He probably was not born deaf, for then he would be the most pitiable of all people. Then he would be unable to read, unable to learn basic skills, and unable to express himself. Now in spite of his speech impediment, he could make himself understood.

Jesus performed a number of actions in healing this handicapped man. After he had taken him aside, he put his fingers into the man's ears; he spat onto his fingertips and with his moistened fingers touched the man's tongue; then he looked up into heaven sighing; and last he commanded, "*Ephphatha!*" which is the Aramaic word for "Be opened!"

These are Jesus' symbolic actions that follow one another meaningfully:

- Taking the man aside in privacy, he makes him more receptive to the miracle that is about to happen.
- Showing that hearing precedes speaking, he points to the opening of the inner ears.
- Touching the man's tongue with moistened fingers, he grants him the gift of fluency.
- Looking up to heaven, he indicates that the miracle of healing comes from God the Father.
- Sighing, Jesus reveals his deep emotions.
- Speaking the man's native language with the word *Ephphatha*, he establishes a verbal bond with him.

These are not magic actions of a miracle-worker who utters his incantations to get results. Jesus's actions were preliminary to the miracle itself, for he used them to communicate with a man who was unable to hear. Then he called on God to make the miracle happen, and by means of an Aramaic word he related directly to the man in his own language. Immediately thereafter the miracle took place.

At the moment the healing happened, the first words the man spoke were addressed to Jesus. We have no knowledge of what was said, but Jesus's directive not to tell anyone was not heeded. There was no stopping the man's desire to tell what had happened to him. As a result, the people who heard him were astonished. In their amazement they praised Jesus by declaring that he was doing everything well. They said that he made the deaf hear and the mute speak.

109

Points to Ponder

- After Jesus cast out a legion of demons from a man in Gadara of the Decapolis, he told him to convey the great things God had done in their midst to his compatriots. But the man who was deaf and mute was told not to say a word. This definitely appears contradictory at first sight. How can a person healed from an inability to hear and speak obey a command not to talk about this to anyone? Possibly Jesus planned to extend his stay in the Decapolis and thus placed more emphasis on preaching the good news than on healing the sick and afflicted.
- Jesus was in Gentile territory where he did not have to fear direct opposition from Jewish clergy. At Jacob's well, the Samaritan woman learned that Jesus was the Messiah, but he did not tell her to be silent. On the contrary, Jesus used her to be his evangelist to the Samaritans. Perhaps he wanted to achieve positive results by giving the man a negative command.
- Today God's messengers who spread the word about Jesus's miracles are fiercely opposed by obstinate skeptics who refuse to accept the message of salvation. To be sure, we admit that the opponents' spiritual ears must be opened, their hardened hearts be broken, their stubborn wills be bent before they become receptive to God's message. Salvation is not the work of human beings but is an act of God. He uses his servants to make the message of salvation known to others.

DEMONS EXPELLED

A Speech-Impaired Man

Matthew 9:32–34

Demon-Possessed and Mute

Among the many people Jesus healed was a man who could not speak. He lived in a world all his own, even though he had the senses of hearing, sight, smell, and touch. Some of the man's relatives or friends had observed Jesus healing the sick, the afflicted, and the demon-possessed. Out of kindness they brought him to Jesus with an unspoken request for healing.

Jesus immediately sensed the presence of a demon in the man, for this evil spirit had caused him to be excluded from the world of speech. This fallen angel at once sensed the divine authority of the Son of God and knew that he had to vacate the deaf-mute man.

When Jesus began his public ministry, Satan released all his demonic angels with instructions to oppose the Son of God and to inflict every known illness and physical disorder on the people. The demons soon realized that they were unable to resist Jesus's power over them. When he spoke, they had to depart. His command was sufficient to send them back to Satan from whom they had come.

As the Son of God, Jesus possessed authority that could not be compared to the power that fallen angels displayed. He was far superior to them, even when demons created disruption among the people and destruction in nature. Appointed by God as the heir of all things, Jesus rules supreme. He merely has to speak a word to fallen angels and, ceasing their destructive work, they depart.

After Jesus cast out the demon, the man afflicted with an inability to speak suddenly began to talk. Now everyone knew that his erratic behavior had to be attributed to a demon, not to a birth defect. All along the demon had prevented the man from speaking and acting normally. But when the demon left the man, the people had tangible proof that Jesus had completely healed him.

The Gospel writer omits the detail on how Jesus drove out the demon, but similar incidents in the Gospel narratives indicate that demons were expelled simply by Jesus' spoken word. Jesus voiced no magic formulas, did not resort to spells, and uttered no chants. He merely spoke and the demons departed.

Jesus had come to free his people from Satan's rule and to establish the kingdom of God on earth. At his command demons had to depart from that kingdom and return to Satan's realm of darkness.

Action and Reaction

As soon as the demon departed and the man began to speak, the crowds that witnessed this miracle were amazed. Countless people were present at the scene and noticed what had happened. Because of the miracles that Jesus performed, crowds in increasing numbers followed him, although many of them were drawn by the novelty rather than spiritual reasons. When they saw Jesus doing miracles, they said to one another: "We have never seen anything like it in Israel."

Since the time of the prophets Elijah and Elisha, and later in the days of Daniel, miracles had not occurred among the Jews. During and after the exile, miracles ceased. But when Jesus appeared on the scene, he performed one miracle after another. Among these wonders, the healing of the mute man was unique. The crowds thought the miracle of casting out a demon that deprived a man of speaking was outstanding. In their eyes it was a top-notch performance—the best in Israel. Later they would see an even more astounding miracle when they witnessed Jesus raising someone from the dead, especially Lazarus who had been buried for four days. That miracle was the best of all.

The Pharisees were not at all elated. Instead of praising God for the wonders worked among them, they were saying that Jesus was the prince of demons and because of that position he had power to cast out demons. They were upset that Jesus gathered multitudes around him while they were left with only a handful of followers. The Pharisees were filled with jealousy and considered Jesus an intruder who had to be demeaned. They gave him the epithet "the prince of demons" to equate him with Satan.

With their knowledge of the Scriptures, the Pharisees should have been the first to recognize Jesus as the Messiah. They should have been rejoicing with the crowds; they should have pointed to Jesus fulfilling messianic prophecies; and they should have told the people that the Messiah was standing in their midst. The Pharisees should have quoted from memory the prophecies that spoke about the Messiah opening the eyes of the blind and unstopping the ears of the deaf. That was their task as religious leaders and teachers of the Law.

Instead the Pharisees presented Jesus as Satan personified. And that was the worst sin they could have committed. Jesus taught that if anyone knew the Scriptures but actively went against them, he committed the sin against the Holy Spirit. Jesus said that sins spoken against the Son of Man would be forgiven, but the sin against the Spirit would not be forgiven in either this world or the next.

All of us fall into sin from time to time, but by confessing our sins we receive God's forgiving grace. On the contrary, all those who deliberately go against the teachings of the Scriptures with full knowledge of them are not forgiven. These people sin against the Holy Spirit and cut themselves off from the living God.

Points to Ponder

- The Gospels indicate that not every deaf or mute person was possessed by a demon. To be sure, there is a difference between a physical handicap and being demon-possessed. We tend to think that a demon causes a person to be insane or engage in uncontrollable acts, but that is not always the case. True, a demon can enter and manipulate an individual and even use the person's tongue to speak. Nonetheless, not all mentally disturbed persons are demon-possessed.

- When Jesus began his ministry, miracles accompanied his preaching and teaching. Also Jesus's apostles had the power to perform signs, wonders, and miracles that served as a witness to the gospel they preached. After the apostles died, their authority to perform miracles also ceased.

- Missionaries who preach the gospel in areas of the world that have not yet come to know Jesus as their Savior can testify to the occurrence of miracles. But in today's Christianized countries where the gospel is regularly preached, no faith healer can instantly restore those people who are both deaf and mute, who have been blind since birth, and whose limbs are withered.

116

- Today there are numerous people with a thorough knowledge of the Scriptures who openly deny and repudiate the Bible's cardinal doctrines. They refuse to accept Jesus's virgin birth, his physical resurrection from the dead, his ascension to heaven, and his promised return. They are like the teachers of the Law and Pharisees in Jesus's day against whom Jesus uttered his woes. He called them blind leaders of the blind. Eventually they would have to face their God and give an account of their words and actions.

A Synagogue Demoniac

Mark 1:21–28; Luke 4:31–37

Evil Spirits

Jesus entered the synagogue of Capernaum where he was invited to teach on a given Sabbath. He had a receptive audience, for the people noticed that his teaching differed from that of the Pharisees, scribes, and teachers of the Law. Whereas the clergy of that day would always pay proper respect to eminent teachers of bygone generations and never speak in their own name, Jesus spoke on his own authority.

Jesus' sermons were true to the Scriptures, filled with suitable and meaningful illustrations that were applicable to daily life. He spoke with authority, power, and conviction in a style that the people appreciated. Indeed he was a master teacher who excelled in every respect. Consequently, the common people heard him gladly.

But Jesus never revealed his true identity to the people, for that would effectively end his ministry. He never revealed to them that he was the Messiah, the Son of God. It was only at his trial when the high priest asked him whether he was the Son of the Blessed One that he openly admitted his true identity of being God's Son. The effect of this admission was the end of his earthly ministry, for the high priest and his associates condemned him to death.

However, whenever Jesus confronted evil spirits, the demons would cry out that he had come to torture them before their time of punishment. They recognized him as the Holy One of God at one occasion and at another instance they identified him as Jesus, Son of the Most High God.

Demons were created as angels, that is, messengers of God. When countless angels revolted against God and fell from their pristine position, they became Satan's messengers. With their leader they continuously rebel against God. Demons submit to Satan, who uses them to advance his kingdom in opposition to God's kingdom. They obey Satan's laws and repudiate God's laws. They induce human beings to be citizens in Satan's kingdom instead of God's kingdom. They enter human beings, distort their personalities, and even speak through them.

Although demons are limited in what they can do, they have knowledge of their fate, namely, their destruction. In Jesus's day, the demons acknowledged him as the Holy One of God. They knew that he was far superior to them and to their master, Satan. They also understood that Jesus had power over them. When Jesus merely spoke a command, they had to leave a demon-possessed person.

Last Word

A man who was possessed by an evil spirit attended the worship service in the synagogue of Capernaum that Sabbath. While Jesus was preaching, the demon within the man cried out, "What do you want with us, Jesus of Nazareth?" Notice the demonic voice used the word *us* to confirm that there were many demons. The voice continued, "Have you come to destroy *us*? I know who you are, the Holy One of God."

These demons confronted Jesus while he was preaching. Instantly they knew that he would cast them out by his divine power. Jesus had come to invade their territory and take it away from them. He had come to bind Satan, the ruler of the demons, and then carry off his possessions.

Not the demon but Jesus had authority, and thus in no uncertain terms he told the demon to be quiet. He did not allow it to reveal his identity because that would limit his ministry. Not Satan its sender, but Jesus the Judge silenced it with a single command, "Be quiet!" In a stern voice he rebuked the demon and ordered it to leave the hapless man.

But the unclean spirit refused to give up without a fight. He took hold of the man by shaking him violently and throwing him to the ground, although without causing harm. Then with a shriek the demon departed.

There is no power in heaven and on earth that is able to resist Jesus's authority. He as God's agent created all angelic beings and has power over them. Although Scripture does not record the creation of angels, we know that at the beginning they were all without sin. After Satan's rebellion against God, one-third of the angels fell with him. All angels, whether they are those who have fallen away from God or those who continue in their pristine state, must obey Jesus's commanding voice. All must submit to him, for he has the final word.

Jesus commanded the demon to be quiet and to come out of the man, and at once the demon obeyed. Just then the miracle of healing occurred as a result of Jesus's divine power. He is the supreme ruler whose voice the demons are unable to ignore and whose power they cannot escape. After his resurrection, Jesus ascended to heaven and took his seat at God's right hand; all angels, authorities, and powers are subject to him.

The demon screeched when it left the body of the man. It let out a hideous sound of defeat and failure. This unclean spirit had met its match and lost, for it would eventually be consigned to hell to await the judgment day.

Astonishment and Wonder

The people who witnessed the casting out of the demon were filled with amazement and looked at both Jesus and the man whom he had healed. They were astonished by the miracle that had taken place before their eyes. They had heard the demon identify Jesus as the Son of God, and they had witnessed him casting out an evil spirit by the power of God. But who was this Jesus of Nazareth?

Those in attendance at the worship service had listened to his teaching, and they had noticed that he proclaimed the truth by coming straight to the point that intersected their lives. He spoke to their hearts about the love of God that was meaningful and heartening.

In addition, Jesus had added the deed to the words he had spoken. He had delivered a man who had been unmanageable and erratic because of an evil spirit that had taken hold of him. And now with a voice of authority, Jesus had healed this unfortunate man and restored him to normal health and a sound mind.

The people asked themselves what kind of teaching Jesus conveyed that demons would leave a person at his command. They saw him as a miracle-worker in whom the Spirit of God dwelled. The news about his teaching and healing ministry spread throughout the land, from mouth to mouth, throughout Galilee and beyond.

Points to Ponder

- Preachers who no longer proclaim the inspired Word of God and deny its cardinal doctrines are told by Jesus to

121

depart from him. He calls them workers of iniquity because they have forfeited their calling as his messengers and have become spokespeople for his opponent. When ambassadors abroad fail to speak for their governments, a summons for their resignation is inevitable. When pastors no longer bring the gospel of Christ, they are not worthy of their calling but face eventual dismissal. Those who reject the deity of Christ show an appalling ignorance that even demons in Jesus's day did not share, for the evil spirits confessed that Jesus is indeed the Son of the Most High God.

- Why does God permit Satan and his cohorts to do their evil work on earth? The answer is that he allows it for his glory. Not Satan but Jesus is the Victor, and we are victorious with him. God is in control in all situations all the time. He denied Satan a place in heaven, caused him to lose the battle against the archangel Michael and his host, and banished him to the earth.

- Satan knows that his days are numbered, even though he continues to vent his wrath against God, his Word, and God's people. Against Satan and his legions, God's judgment is unerring and inescapable. Satan is a five-time loser. He tried to kill the baby Jesus in Bethlehem, but Joseph with Mary and the baby left for Egypt. Jesus ascended to heaven and Satan tried to follow him, but he had to fight a war with the archangel Michael and lost. Satan fights the church, the body of Christ, but thus far he has been unable to eliminate God's people. Satan spreads falsehood throughout the world, but truth eventually catches up with him. And last, he tries to conquer those people who hold to the truth of God's Word and the testimony of Jesus, and Satan loses again.

The Demoniac in Gadara

Matthew 8:28–34; Mark 5:1–20; Luke 8:26–39

From Bad to Worse

Jesus and his disciples were crossing the Lake of Galilee but were caught in a violent storm that suddenly appeared. The storm was so fierce that the disciples began to fear for their safety. As the wind blew and the water splashed across the boat, Jesus was sound asleep in the stern. After an intensive day of teaching and healing the people, he was physically exhausted. It was obvious that his mind and body needed rest.

The scared-stiff disciples shook Jesus awake because their lives were in danger. He stood up and commanded the waves and the wind to be still. All at once there was a perfect calm—no wind and placid water.

Soon afterward the disciples and Jesus moored on the east side of the lake. They disembarked and entered the countryside known as Gentile territory. This became evident when they discerned a large herd of pigs feeding in the lush grass on a hillside that bordered a cemetery with underground caves. The Jews considered pigs unclean animals and therefore could not go near them.

Almost instantly the disciples noticed a demon-possessed man wild and unclothed rushing toward them. The Gospel of Matthew relates that there were two men. The Gospels of Mark and Luke refer to one man, who was the spokesman for the other one.

The disciples had just faced the tempest on the lake, and now they faced the tempest of a fierce man with enormous physical strength. Jesus had shown them violence in nature on the lake; now he made them encounter demonic power on land.

No doubt the disciples asked themselves why Jesus had wanted to cross the lake, enter a foreign region, and expose them to physical harm. Could he who stilled the storm also subdue this violent man? By themselves they were unable to cope with this man. Hence they hid behind Jesus, so to speak, because he had the power and authority to cast out demons.

My Name Is Legion

This ferocious man did not live in a house, for the citizens of that town had banished him to dwell in an underground graveyard among the tombs. He was too much of an embarrassment to the public, especially when he walked around in public unclothed and screeching at the top of his voice at all hours of the day and night. The people were at a loss and did not know what to do with this man because no one was able to subdue him. On top of all this, he used sharp stones to cut himself. He was an awful sight, was filthy, and had a repulsive odor.

When capable men chained the demon-possessed man hand and foot, he always broke loose. There was no way to confine him in the underground burial ground because his strength was phenomenal due to the demons who made their home in his body. They gave him incomparable power at the expense of the man's physical body. They drove him away from the town and into solitary places of the hill country.

When the demon-possessed man saw Jesus coming ashore, he ran toward him as fast as he could and fell on his knees in front of him. The disciples were fearful but trusted that Jesus would be able to control him and protect them from harm.

The demons drove the man toward Jesus. They were like moths at night, drawn to the fire and then getting scorched. They were the ones who recognized Jesus and knew that he would cast them out of the man and send them back to Satan.

Not the man but one of the demons speaking through his mouth shouted at the top of his voice, "What do you want with me, Jesus, Son of the Most High God? I beg you in the name of God do not torment me." The demon was fully aware of Jesus's identity and responded to Jesus's command to come out of the man. But the demon begged him in the name of God not to hand it over to be tortured prior to the day of judgment, that is, before the appointed time of the final judgment. The demon, however, was powerless in the presence of the divine Son of God and knew that it had to submit to him.

Jesus sensed that this demon was not alone and thus asked, "What is your name?" The demon said, "My name is Legion, for we are many." The word *legion* was used in the Roman military to signify a group of six thousand men. The term symbolizes enormous strength and numbers of demonic power. Here is a picture of a demonic army residing in a single person that confronted Jesus the Son of God, who had invaded their territory.

Note that before Jesus's public ministry began, Satan had taken him to a high place and offered him all the kingdoms of the world. He tempted him by saying that if he would worship Satan, the devil would give him all the world's splendor and authority. But Jesus refused and told his adversary to worship God and serve him only. Now Jesus invaded Satan's kingdom and drove a legion of demons out of a man. Not Satan but Jesus is Conqueror and King in God's kingdom.

The demons implored Jesus not to send them back to the Abyss, namely, the bottomless pit where they were destined to suffer eternal punishment. They wanted to lengthen their stay on this earth a little while longer and thus postpone that awful judgment day.

Two Thousand Pigs

Again and again the demons begged Jesus not to send them outside of that region. Satan had assigned them to stay in that particular area among the graves, the dead, and the skeletons. They shied away from bondage in the bottomless pit and pleaded with Jesus to send them instead into a large herd of some two thousand pigs that were grazing along the hillside.

Jesus granted their request to enter the pigs, with the result that the whole herd, now demon-possessed, rushed down the hillside all the way to the edge of the cliff and plunged headlong into the water of the Lake of Galilee. And even though pigs are good swimmers, all of them drowned.

Demons reportedly reside in waterless places, but now they find themselves in a watery grave—a form of punishment. Nonetheless, eternal punishment awaits them at the end of time.

Why did Jesus permit this destruction of life and the ruin of the local economy? In doing so he created a growing animosity of the Gentiles toward the Jews. The citizens of Gadara saw him as a Jew who had taken their livelihood away in an apparent attempt to convert them to the Jewish faith.

A few considerations are in order. Jesus healed one of the Gentiles by setting him free from demonic oppression and restoring him to normal health. He dispatched the demons, who left the region when they entered the water. It is true that he deprived a number of people of gainful employment, but he wanted them to see the change that had occurred in one of their own citizens. Although the Gentiles knew that the Jews regarded pigs as unclean animals, Jesus did not intend to make Jews out of the people who depended on the income of raising, slaughtering, and marketing pigs.

Jesus's main objectives were to

- liberate a human being from Satan's clutches,
- have him become a useful citizen,
- instruct him to tell his people about God's goodness, and
- make the Gentiles appreciate the value of a human being.

In addition, the population had to acknowledge that someone endowed with divine power had broken the stranglehold of demons residing in the man. They had to admit the difference between being demon-possessed on the one hand and being freed by Jesus on the other hand.

In their midst stood the great miracle-worker, who could teach the people about the love of God and show them the way of salvation. They witnessed that in their midst Jesus had performed a miracle—no ordinary feat. Here was a human being endowed with divine authority that was far greater than the power of demons. Here was a man who could perform miracles. He could heal their sick, give sight to the blind and hearing to the deaf, make the lame walk, cleanse their lepers, and show them the way to God.

The herdsmen fled into the town and to the country-side. There they reported what had happened. As a result, the people came to the spot where Jesus, the disciples, and the former demoniac were. The demon-possessed man was sitting there clothed and in his right mind. The demons who had made their dwelling in the man had gone into the pigs that had rushed to their death in the lake. There was a restoration spiritually speaking, for the demons had left their area.

Dismiss the Healer

Although not appreciated by the Gentiles, Jesus had helped them see that the physical and spiritual healing of a human being was of far greater value than the cost of a herd of pigs. By means of the miracle, he was teaching them that the redeeming love of God is infinitely better than the cruel enslavement of Satan. The people had the evidence right in front of them. They saw the messenger from God standing in their midst. He who healed the demoniac had the power to bring spiritual salvation and physical healing to all of them.

The herdsmen and the disciples were eyewitnesses to what had occurred and told the people about Jesus's majesty and sovereign power. Also the man who was healed testified about Jesus's liberating authority over the demonic world. All Jesus wanted from the people was a demonstration of their willingness to learn from him.

This was not to be, for the citizens of that area considered their financial loss of greater significance than their spiritual healing. To prevent any other calamities happening in their midst, they asked Jesus to leave their district. They saw him as an intruder who had deprived them of their financial income. He had upset their economy by reducing their livestock to zero and causing severe unemployment among the workers. In short, they placed their material interests above their spiritual needs.

The man who was at the center of the incident noticed the refusal of the townspeople to have Jesus stay with them. As a result, he went to Jesus and asked if he might accompany him. Undoubtedly the man wanted to express his thankfulness to his benefactor. He was of the opinion that he could do this better by accompanying Jesus than by staying with his own people.

However, Jesus saw the matter differently. He told the man to return home and tell all the people about the great things Jesus had done for him. The man could express his gratitude by being a missionary for Jesus so that the love of God might become evident among the Gentiles. Jesus had turned the man from satanic darkness to the light of God's kingdom. By staying with his relatives and fellow citizens he could lead them to the knowledge of God and the possession of eternal salvation.

Points to Ponder

- Often people with or without knowledge of the Bible say, "Money is the root of all evil." But this is quoting Scripture incorrectly. In effect it says, "For the *love of money* is a root of all kinds of evil." Money by itself is not wicked, for God continually blesses his people with bounteous supplies of material goods. Persons who have a propensity for amassing wealth are prone to fall into the trap of making money their god instead of worshiping God who has provided their resources. They fail to love God with heart, soul, mind, and strength because money has become their idol. The consequences are that they reap a harvest of griefs as the devil leads them astray.

- How does a Christian oppose satanic forces? Satan comes in the form of either the deceiver or the destroyer. He employs the weapons of both pretense and violence. Some people are completely in his power, and thus they oppose God, his Word, and his people. They want to see a complete separation between religion and public life. They have banned God and Scripture from the public square.
- However, God does not leave his people defenseless in a world dominated by the evil one. Paul instructs Christians to put on seven pieces of spiritual armor to withstand the wiles of the devil. He says, "Put on the shoes of peace, so that you can be God's peacemakers. Put on the belt of truth to counteract the lie. Wear the breastplate of righteousness to fight the forces of injustice. Take in hand the shield of faith to withstand the fiery darts of Satan. Hold the sword of the Spirit in the other hand, and wield it in your defense. Don the helmet of salvation in the knowledge that you are victorious in Christ. And last, pray constantly to Jesus, the captain of God's army, who will direct you and keep you safe" (Eph. 6:13–18).
- While the subjects of Satan bear his signature on their foreheads and hands, Christians wear the seal of baptism in the name of the Father, the Son, and the Holy Spirit. This allows us as God's children to come to the Father in prayer and ask him to protect us from the onslaughts of the evil one. We call on the name of the Son and point to the baptismal seal on our foreheads. We ask him to be our big brother and watch over us so that we do not go astray. And we implore the Holy Spirit to fill us with wisdom and power to overcome temptation and pass the test in times of trials. The result is that God answers our prayer.

THE CANAANITE MOTHER

Matthew 15:21–28; Mark 7:24–30

Ministry Abroad

The Great Commission tells us to make disciples of all nations by baptizing them and by teaching them everything that Jesus has commanded. But did Jesus during his ministry apply that principle to himself? When he commissioned his disciples to go on their first missionary tour, he told them not to go to the Gentiles and the Samaritans but to "the lost sheep of Israel." Yet Jesus went into the Gentile area of Gadara, and on another occasion he healed the servant of a Roman centurion. At one time during his ministry, Jesus with his disciples went beyond Israel's borders and entered the region of Tyre and Sidon.

Why did Jesus go abroad? The answer may very well be that numerous people from the Phoenician coastline had come to Israel to hear Jesus preach and to bring him their sick to be healed. It may also be that he had to leave Israel because of increasing opposition to his preaching and teaching. For his own safety he went for some rest and relaxation to the city of Tyre. This was about a forty-mile (sixty-kilometer) journey from Capernaum traveling around the base of Mount Hermon.

When Jesus and his disciples entered the coastal city of Tyre, he rented lodgings and tried to stay incognito. He wanted to be alone with his disciples and prepare them for what lay in store for him in the future. They had to know that he would be apprehended, face trials, and be executed. After his death he would rise from the grave on the third day.

To keep thirteen men undercover was impossible because their speech and apparel betrayed them. Some people who had listened to Jesus in Galilee recognized him. The news about Jesus being in town spread like wildfire: "The Great Physician is here!"

A mother whose daughter was suffering from demon possession heard about Jesus's presence. She was of Greek descent and was born in Syrian Phoenicia, now known as Lebanon. She was a Gentile who spoke both Greek and Aramaic and had lived in the city for some time.

This woman had to overcome many barriers:

- She was a Gentile rather than a Jew.
- She was a woman and therefore not allowed to speak to a man who was not a relative.
- She was living in a pagan culture that worshiped heathen deities.

The woman knew that medical doctors in her city were unable to help her ailing child, but she was confident that Jesus could heal her. She knew that Jews looked down on Gentiles and that she as a female might not be heard. However, the need of the hour was stronger than her hesitation to approach Jesus and address him.

132

This Syro-Phoenician woman addressed Jesus as Lord, which may have been politeness but may also have implied respect for his divinity. She identified him as the Son of David, which among the Jews was the equivalent of calling him "Messiah." Her choice of words in addressing Jesus reveals her elementary faith in God. She kept on asking him to cast a demon out of her daughter because the girl was suffering terribly.

We would expect Jesus to show this woman kindness, compassion, and a readiness to help. Instead, he acted as if he did not hear her. No wonder, therefore, that the disciples had had enough of her imposition on the Master's time. They asked him to send her away, because all the while she continued to repeat her request.

Faith That Triumphs

Why did Jesus appear to drive the Syro-Phoenician woman away? He wanted to test the woman's faith and see whether it was genuine. At the same time it was a lesson for the disciples to note that faith supersedes racial and national boundaries. They had heard Jesus say to them when he healed the centurion's servant, "I have not found such great faith even in Israel." And here in Sidon they would observe the faith of a Canaanite woman.

Jesus told the woman that it was not right to take food offered to children and toss it to the little dogs. The implied message to her was clear: Gentiles need not apply! The expression *children* refers to the Jewish people who were in God's covenant. And the reference to dogs compared non-Jews to little house dogs that consumed bits and pieces of food that fell off the table at mealtime. Jesus's words were far from complimentary; his attitude toward her seemed discourteous.

The Syro-Phoenician woman was rejected and would have to go back home. But is not Jesus the Savior of the world, regardless of anyone's status and background? The Jews called this woman a Canaanite because the early Phoenicians identified themselves by that name. They were the original dwellers in the land. But the Jews used the term to reject a Gentile of that region.

Even so, the woman's faith proved to be rock solid, for she immediately replied to Jesus's comment that the bread of children would not be tossed to house dogs. She responded, "Yes, Lord, but even the dogs eat the crumbs that fall from their master's table." Her determination was admirable in spite of Jesus's reference to dogs. She was not to be marginalized, and her unflinching determination was obvious.

The woman boldly asked Jesus whether that which Jews reject could be a blessing to Gentiles. If little dogs can eat kosher bread, might not Gentiles eat that food too?

If Jesus would be willing to accept Gentiles, then these people could no longer be called dogs. They would then be recipients of his grace and mercy and would be drawn into the circle of God's covenant people. The woman's faith triumphed.

Jesus was astonished and exclaimed, "Woman, great is your faith! Go home for the demon has left your daughter." The mother rushed home to her daughter, saw her lying on the bed, and noticed that the demon had departed from her. She was healed and back to normal.

Without entering her house, Jesus had healed the woman's daughter from a distance. By doing so he would not offend Jewish sensitivities and hesitation to enter Gentile homes. At other occasions involving healing miracles of non-Jews, he abstained from coming into their dwellings. To illustrate, he healed the servant of a Roman centurion without going into his house, and while he was in Cana, he merely said to a royal official, although of Jewish origin, that his child in Capernaum was restored to health.

134

Jesus's power to perform miracles could not be hindered by time and space. As Lord of lords and King of kings he had full control over demonic angels. Without Jesus even speaking a word, fallen angels had to submit to him and leave the bodies and minds of those whom they had afflicted with life-threatening ailments.

Points to Ponder

- The apostle Paul exemplifies the theme of Jews and Gentiles by writing about the branches of an olive tree that are broken off because of unbelief while wild olive branches are grafted into a cultivated olive tree because of faith. This procedure seems to go contrary to nature. But note that Jesus performed miracles among his own people, who rejected him, and he reached out to Gentiles, who acknowledged him with unfeigned faith.

- When Jesus tested the Syro-Phoenician woman's faith, his attitude toward her seemed at first unaccommodating and disinterested. His negative attitude, however, clearly outlined the extent of her faith in him. He purposefully used the adjective *great* to describe her trust. This illustrates that we are frequently put to the test when God wants us to exercise patience. As stars shine most brightly in the darkest of nights, so our faith excels in the severest of circumstances.

- The Book of Acts clearly reveals that the love of Jesus broke down racial barriers between Jews and Gentiles. With the spread of the gospel, increasing multitudes of Gentiles have entered the church. Today Christians circle the globe and are present everywhere.

- Do our non-Christian neighbors see that we love Jesus by the love and respect we show them? We know that

Christ's love transcends all barriers of race, color, language, and nationality. Thus, our actions should speak louder than our words in being his messenger to others around us. We don't have to go to mission fields to acquaint people with the claims of Christ when they are living next door to us. People observe Christians every day because we are living, figuratively, in glass houses.

THE EPILEPTIC BOY
WITH A DEMON

Matthew 17:14–19; Mark 9:14–29; Luke 9:37–42

The Transfiguration

Jesus took Peter, John, and James to the top of Mount Hermon to give them a glimpse of heaven. His purpose for taking these three disciples to the mountaintop was to show them his transfiguration in heavenly glory. There they saw Jesus transfigured in glorious light in the presence of Moses and Elijah. Then the voice of God the Father spoke: "This is my Son whom I love and with whom I am pleased. Listen to him!"

Peter never forgot this experience. Decades later when he was writing one of his Epistles he repeated the words God had spoken. This event was used in a powerful way in the lives of these three disciples as their eyes were opened so they could begin to comprehend Jesus's death, resurrection, and ascension.

Here is a contrast of heaven and earth. The evangelists picture Jesus with his inner circle of Peter, James, and John on a high mountain where he had gone to pray and where he was transfigured. The three disciples saw Jesus with Moses and Elijah in heavenly splendor. But when Jesus and the disciples came down from the mountain, they immediately were confronted by a boy possessed by a demon. Here Satan, whom Jesus called the prince of this world, made his presence known as the adversary.

Demon Possession

While Peter and his two associates had a mountaintop experience of seeing a glimpse of heaven, at the foot of the mountain the nine other disciples were coping with a demonic power that refused to depart. A father had come to them with his epileptic son, who was possessed by a demon. But the disciples were unable to help. They tried their level best to cast out the demon, but it was all to no avail. All of them confessed failure and had to yield to the power of a demon in full control. The only thing they could do was wait for Jesus to come down from the mountain.

In this incident three parties played a leading role: the father with his ailing son, the disciples who were incapable of casting out the demon, and Jesus, who took control of the situation. For a long time a father and a mother had been forced to watch their son going through epileptic seizures. Soon they realized that a demon had taken up permanent residence in their son. They noticed that this evil power would cause convulsions that led to foaming at the mouth, a rigidity of the body, and the gnashing of teeth. This demon was intent on causing physical harm to their son to the point of trying to kill him by casting him into fire or water. If it had not been for the vigilance of both father and mother, the demon would have succeeded.

The father had heard about the miracles Jesus had performed in Galilee and elsewhere, restoring the sick to vibrant health. He wondered whether Jesus would be willing to heal his son by casting out the demon. He still had reservations, but necessity forced him to take his son to the Galilean healer.

When the two arrived at the place where Jesus had been, the father was told that the Great Physician was on Mount Hermon with three of his disciples. He boldly asked the nine disciples to exorcise the demon. But after a few attempts by one or more of the disciples, he found that they were incapable of helping him and his son.

First Andrew had uttered a foolproof formula in casting out demons: "In the name of Jesus of Nazareth, I tell you, come out of the boy." Nothing happened. Then Bartholomew wanted to exorcise the demon. He used the same words Andrew had uttered, but again the result was nil.

As the disciples were trying to deal with their failure, they had to endure the biting ridicule of some teachers of the Jewish religious Law. These people were mocking the nine disciples for their inability to drive out evil spirits. Even though the disciples reminded their hecklers of earlier times when they had indeed had the power to cast out demons, they felt defeated on two fronts. They had to cope with both human ridicule as well as satanic control over an epileptic boy.

Jesus's Arrival

When Jesus came down from the mountain, he noticed that a large crowd of people surrounded the nine disciples who were being harassed by the teachers of the Law. The people were astonished at Jesus' sudden appearance at a critical moment when the devil seemed to be in full control and the disciples powerless. They came running toward him and greeted him.

Jesus asked the teachers of the Law what they were arguing about with his disciples. In a sense, he placed a protective arm around his embattled men, who looked up to him as their captain. None of the learned lawyers dared to speak up, and their ridicule suddenly came to an end. They did not have the courage to tell Jesus that they had scorned the disciples.

Then a person in the crowd spoke up and told Jesus that he had brought his son to him because an evil spirit had deprived the boy of the ability to speak. The demon would attack the son, cast him to the ground, make him foam at the mouth, grind his teeth, and cause him to become stiff. The boy suffered from both epileptic attacks and demonic assaults. The father had petitioned Jesus's disciples to cast out the demon; they had tried but failed.

Jesus addressed his disciples and rebuked them for their lack of faith and asked them how long he had to stay in their midst and put up with them. Would they ever be able to be his representatives when they could not even cast out a demon? Jesus ordered them to bring the boy to him.

In the presence of Jesus, the demon threw the boy into convulsions, cast him to the ground, and made him roll around foaming at the mouth. The father informed Jesus about these violent demonic attacks and pleaded for help and mercy. He showed that he had faith even though it was feeble.

Jesus spoke words of encouragement by saying to the father, "If you are sure it can be done for you, then know that all things can be done for the one who believes." The father promptly responded with a spiritual affirmation and an appeal, "I believe; please help my unbelief." His words implied a request for continued help to strengthen his faith that was being assailed by doubt.

Then as the crowd was running toward him, Jesus rebuked the evil spirit. He said, "You spirit that keeps the boy from talking and hearing, I order you to come out of him and never to enter him again." The demon obeyed and left, but not without screaming and causing the boy to fall and roll around. As a result the boy looked as if he were dead. But Jesus took him by the hand, raised him, and made him stand on his feet.

The conflict between a demonic spirit and Jesus's omnipotence came to an end when the miracle of restoration occurred. Jesus served as God's agent when he created the angels. Therefore, he as their Creator has authority even over fallen angels; they have to submit to him when he orders them to depart. Satan as the master of demons is unable to overrule Jesus, for he too has to submit to him.

In private afterward, the disciples asked Jesus why they could not cast out this demon. They had done so on other occasions, but this time they had failed miserably. They admitted defeat but wanted to know why they had not succeeded. In addition to faith, what else would they need? Then Jesus told them that this kind of demon could be cast out only in answer to prayer. That is, the disciples should have asked God the Father to give them authority and power to exorcise this evil spirit.

Points to Ponder

- Jesus said more than once that if we have faith like a mustard seed, we can move mountains. The mustard seed is the smallest of garden seeds, and mountains are massive obstacles on life's pathway. Yet these obstacles can be overcome in faith. Faith and prayer go hand in hand and should never be treated as separate entities.

- Many times our efforts to serve God result in failure, and then we wonder what went wrong. The answer often lies in our failure to pray to God and seek his will. We are like Jonah, who first ran away from God

141

by boarding a ship; then in the belly of a whale he ran toward God in prayer; in Nineveh he ran with God; and last, after he had preached in Nineveh, he tried to run ahead of God by telling him what to do.

- For every evil spirit in this world there are two good angels to guide and protect us. This does not mean that we should pray to an angel or to a believer who has passed on to glory. We pray to God, who is the giver of every good and perfect gift. He grants us power and ability in answer to prayer that is offered in faith.

- By means of modern medicine, epilepsy today is a manageable disease that no longer poses as much of a threat to human beings as it once did. Does our knowledge of these drugs diminish our appreciation for Jesus performing a miracle? Of course not. Jesus cast out an evil spirit that prevented the boy from speaking and hearing. He immediately knew that he faced a demonic power. Epilepsy itself was secondary.

MARY MAGDALENE

Luke 8:1—3; John 20:1—2, 10—18

Devoted Women

Jesus went from towns and villages to places throughout the countryside preaching the good news of God's kingdom. Wherever he went, he not only preached the good news, but he also healed people stricken with numerous illnesses. He confronted the works of Satan in men and women who were demon-possessed. These sufferers, who had no one to help them out of their misery, turned to Jesus.

During Jesus's earthly ministry, Satan seemed to have unleashed countless evil spirits to oppose his labors. The demons, however, immediately realized when they met Jesus that his was a supernatural force they were unable to thwart. A single word from him was sufficient to banish them from the scene with the warning never to return.

While traveling with the twelve disciples, Jesus instructed them in the mysteries of the kingdom. Some of these men were people with sufficient funds such as the fishermen Peter, Andrew, James, and John. Matthew, the former tax collector, was probably well-to-do. Even so, the expenses for the daily upkeep of thirteen men called for additional support.

Some women provided for the daily needs of Jesus and his followers out of their resources. He had met these women at a time when they were suffering of demon possession and other ailments and had healed them. Hence, in an effort to express gratitude to him, they readily gave of their assets to cover the expenses Jesus incurred.

In contrast to the culture of that day where only men followed a teacher, Jesus attracted both men and women in his company. The New Testament mentions some women who honored Jesus by caring for him. Although the men fled, the women were present at the cross. Not the men but the women were the first at the tomb on the day of Jesus's resurrection. Women were present in the upper room when the disciples came together to choose a successor to Judas Iscariot. And women are listed as helpers of the apostles as Paul indicates in his Epistles.

Some men turned against Jesus: Peter rejected Jesus by disowning him three times, and Judas went to the chief priests to betray his Master for thirty pieces of silver. By contrast, the women faithfully followed, defended, and supported Jesus.

Mary of Magdala

Among the women who ministered to Jesus was Mary Magdalene, whose name indicates she was from the town of Magdala situated on the southwest shore of the Lake of Galilee. When Jesus met her, she was known as a demon-possessed woman. Jesus had pity on her, cast out seven demons, and restored her to normal health. Hers was a severe case of demon possession, because the number *seven* describes completeness, that is, she was thoroughly afflicted by these demons. There is no evidence at all that she was an immoral woman or that she had an improper relationship with Jesus.

After Mary regained her mental health, she demonstrated devotion and faithfulness to her benefactor. With other women who had been healed by Jesus, she followed her Master and supported him from her own resources. Two of the other women were Joanna, who was the wife of Herod's business manager, and Susanna.

Mary was devoted to Jesus; she followed him on his last journey to Jerusalem. When his disciples forsook him at the cross, Mary was there with other women to watch him suffer and die. She observed where Joseph of Arimathea and Nicodemus buried Jesus so that she could go to the tomb after the Sabbath was over, early on the morning of the first day of the week. With other women she brought spices to anoint the body of Jesus.

Coming to the burial place, the women discussed how to remove the heavy round stone in front of the entrance to the tomb. When they arrived, they saw that the stone had been rolled away. The soldiers who were supposed to stand on guard were gone.

Mary quickly glanced in and noticed that the tomb was empty. She rushed back into the city of Jerusalem and told Peter and John the news of Jesus's disappearance. Then she returned to the grave where she stood weeping. But through her tear-filled eyes she noticed someone standing there who asked her why she was weeping and for whom she was looking. Mary mistakenly identified him as the gardener. When Jesus called her by name, she recognized his voice. Filled with joy she clasped her arms around him. But he told her not to hold on to him, because he would return to the Father. He instructed her to go to the disciples with the news that he would ascend to heaven. She obeyed and gave them the news that she had seen the resurrected Lord.

145

Points to Ponder

- Devotion to Jesus must always be characterized by a grateful response to him for his constant love and abundant provisions for his people. Whenever these favors are taken for granted, loyalty to the giver of these gifts begins to wane and eventually ceases. Neglecting the virtue of expressing gratitude inevitably results in detached desertion.

- Women express their loyalty to Jesus by fulfilling numerous roles in the ministry of the church. They take leading positions in the social and educational areas and utilize their God-given talents in Christ's service. There is plenty of work that needs to be done in the life of the church, and women fill that need with the talents God has given them.

- The word *devotion* means being an ardent follower and servant of Jesus Christ by obeying his command and expressing undying love to him in thankfulness.

Raised from the Dead

THE WIDOW'S SON AT NAIN

Luke 7:11–16

An Only Son

Death is all around us, for the tears are hardly dry in one family before they start flowing in the next. Behind every obituary flows a flood of tears, and every tombstone is a monument of sorrow. Death reigns supreme until it is defeated as the last enemy.

A widow lived in the little town of Nain located near the southern border of Galilee not far from Samaria. She had lost her husband due to an accident or illness. From time to time she visited his grave in the cemetery on the outskirts of town. She was left with only one son, who became her breadwinner and sole support in her daily needs. Although the empty spot of her departed husband remained, she took great comfort in the presence of her son.

Then one day death struck again and took away her son. Not only was her source of income gone, but much more the intimacy and love of a mother and son had come to an abrupt end. She was overwhelmed by grief, for now she would have to go through life alone.

Even though relatives, friends, and people in the town tried to comfort the widow, they could do nothing to take away her grief. The widow knew that they would soon forget her sorrow when they went on with their own lives. She would have to face the daily grind of loneliness and poverty until death eventually ended her life. No one could remove her sorrow, and no one could alleviate her pain.

The One and Only Son

In Israel funerals were held customarily on the day of death or the next day. Family and friends helped the mother with preparations. Then at the appointed hour the funeral procession left the widow's house on the way to the burial grounds. In Galilee it was expected that the grieving mother would walk at the head of the procession followed by young men carrying the bier with the body of the deceased. Behind that a large crowd of people with hired mourners and flute players brought the array to a close. If a group of people met a funeral procession, they were respectfully obliged to accompany the mourners on the way to the cemetery.

Providentially, just as Jesus, his disciples, and a large crowd of followers came to the town, the funeral procession was coming out. But instead of silently taking his place at the end of the cortege, Jesus first addressed the grieving mother with a word of comfort by telling her not to weep. He fully understood the widow's overwhelming waves of sorrow and took pity on her. Then he nodded to the young men to put down the bier and stop. All eyes were now fixed on Jesus, for who dared to interfere with a funeral? They were curious. The incident itself took their minds off the widow's inconsolable grief.

Jesus touched the bier and then said in a commanding voice for everyone to hear, "Young man, I say to you: Get up!" Here was the one and only Son of God who ordered the only son of the widow to rise from the dead. Here the source of life confronted the angel of death and told it to release its grip on the young man. While others had spoken comforting words to the widow, Jesus not only comforted her, he also acted. He told her son to rise and return.

This was the first miracle of Jesus calling a dead person back to life. The other two were the daughter of Jairus and Lazarus. This was not a resuscitation of a person who appeared to be dead; it was a physical resurrection. Only Jesus as the Son of God was able to perform this unique miracle.

Some of the mourners had heard and seen Jesus heal the sick and the handicapped, but they had not witnessed him calling the dead back to life. This deed was unique, and everyone wondered what would happen next. Yet they were acquainted with the history of their people. The two miracle-working prophets Elijah and Elisha had each raised to life an only son. God is not a God of the dead but of the living.

No sooner did the young man receive the command to sit up, when to the amazement of everyone in the funeral gathering the dead man came back to life. He sat up and immediately began to talk to prove that he was really alive. As Elijah and Elisha respectively gave back to their mothers two boys raised to life, so Jesus handed the grief-stricken widow her son.

The crowd spontaneously burst into praising God and saying that a Great Prophet had come among them to show that God indeed helped his people. They were correct to call Jesus a Great Prophet; he fulfilled the messianic prophecy that God would raise up a prophet like Moses, who was considered the greatest in the history of Israel.

The news of Jesus calling a dead person back to life spread like wildfire throughout the land of the Jews. Nothing like it had ever happened in their recent history. The widow had her son back, sorrow had turned into joy, tears were dried, and laughter was heard. She was a mother again, and her continued support was sure.

Points to Ponder

- The Apostles' Creed speaks in personal terms about the resurrection. Every true Christian faithfully recites the words, "I believe in the resurrection of the body." That is, soul and body will be reunited at the day of Christ's return.
- Of all the world religions only Christianity has a full-fledged doctrine of the resurrection. The apostles in the first century preached this tenet as the basis of the Christian faith. Throughout the centuries, this religious tenet has made Christianity unique.
- One of the hallmarks of the Christian religion is to care for widows and orphans. Whenever Christians devote themselves to caring for these needy people, God accepts their religion as pure and faultless.

The Daughter of Jairus

Matthew 9:18–26; Mark 5:21–43; Luke 8:40–56

An Only Daughter

A man by the name of Jairus lived in the town of Capernaum, where he served as ruler of the local synagogue. For many years he and his wife had faced the prospect of childlessness until they were gladdened by the birth of their only child, a daughter. But after twelve years of happiness in that small family circle, the daughter became very ill. Medical help was either inadequate or not available. She was at the point of death, and Jairus went to look for Jesus as a last resort to find help for her. His faith was strong, for even when he knew in his heart that his daughter could die any moment, he trusted Jesus to come and bring her back to life.

Jairus left the house in a hurry and went to the waterfront where he heard that Jesus was aboard a fishing vessel and could return to shore any time. Yet every moment was precious to the father of this dying child. Then he saw the fishing boat land and Jesus disembarking. He rushed to Jesus. On bended knee he implored him to come to his house immediately to restore his daughter and rescue her from impending death.

The synagogue ruler trusted Jesus to heal his precious child, but his faith was severely tried. As Jesus started to go with him, he was stopped by a woman who had been ill for twelve years due to a blood disorder. Even though Jesus healed her on the spot, the interruption made Jairus despondent. Would the Master be in time to do his daughter any good?

While Jesus talked to the woman, who was now healed and filled with joy, friends of Jairus brought the sad news that his only child had passed away. The news was devastating. Then these friends told him not to bother Jesus any longer. The time for mourning had begun, which meant that special mourners and flute players were hired and funeral arrangements were being made.

Jesus heard the news that the friends had brought Jairus. He was fully aware of the situation but exuded confidence and assurance in the presence of the synagogue ruler. He gave hope and assurance when he said to Jairus, "Don't fear, only believe."

Jairus had shown faith when he went to the harbor with his request for help. He believed that the only person who could help him was Jesus. Now the Teacher told him not to fear but to keep on believing.

The fact that death had entered the family circle of Jairus made it difficult for him to believe and not be afraid. He knew that Jesus could heal the sick, because there were several people in Capernaum Jesus had brought back to normal health: a paralytic, the child of an official, the servant of a centurion, and the woman who had a blood disorder. Nevertheless, he thought that his case was different; his daughter was dead. Would Jesus, who had healed many people, be able to raise a person from death to life?

Jesus understood what was going on in the mind of Jairus and without delay led him out of his grief. He told Jairus not

154

to listen to his friends and the sad news they had brought. Now the time had come to place full confidence in Jesus.

Fear in the face of death is understandable, but to have faith in the face of fear is commendable. When Jairus brought Jesus to his home, the paid mourners and flute players had already arrived and were engaged in loud wailing and beating of chests. Instantly, Jesus took control of the situation and did not allow anyone to enter the house except Peter, John, and James together with the father and mother of the child.

Little Girl, Get Up!

The noise had been excessive, but when Jesus appeared everyone became quiet. He asked the mourners and musicians why they were bawling and wailing. He simply told them, "The child is not dead but asleep." His words caused peals of laughter, for they knew that she was dead. At the same time, their hilarity demonstrated their insincerity and revealed that their sadness was just an outward show.

Jesus, the girl's parents, and three disciples entered the bedroom where the girl was lying. Then Jesus took hold of her hand and said in the Aramaic language that was spoken in the home, *Talitha koum!* which means "Little girl, I say to you, get up!" Then the miracle of the resurrection occurred in the privacy of that bedroom. Jesus, who is the way, the truth, and the life, granted life to this young girl. Although this gift of life would end when death eventually came once more, for the present she again made the family circle complete.

The miracle that took place at the house of Jairus displayed Jesus's power over death and the grave. Satan and his evil angels did not have the final word over life and death, but Jesus the life giver possessed absolute authority. His command uttered in simple wording to the twelve-year-old daughter was sufficient to bring her back to life. He did not speak magical formulas, he uttered no incantations, and he did not wave a wand. He merely told the daughter of Jairus to get up.

The prophets Elijah and Elisha each brought a boy back to life by praying to God and by lying on top of the corpse. They did this more than once, and the dead came back to life. By contrast Jesus did not pray, did not touch the dead body, but only spoke and the young girl came back to life. This was not a reanimation of a physical body that was still alive. It was a miracle performed by Jesus, the author and sustainer of life, the Son of God, the Ruler of the universe.

Jesus told the parents two things: not to tell anyone about the miracle that had happened, and to give the little girl something to eat. The command not to inform the people about what happened sounds incongruous. As soon as she left the bedroom, relatives, friends, and neighbors would see the girl, and the news would spread. However, Jesus did not want this miracle to become widely known and thus hinder him in his work that already was being hampered by the religious authorities.

The instruction to give the girl something to eat was meant to indicate that she should resume a normal life of eating and drinking. The days of her illness had come to an end, and now she again could carry on her daily activities. Jesus governed the supernatural act of raising her from the dead as well as the natural activity of making her eat and drink.

Points to Ponder

- The angel of death is a formidable power that no mortal being can escape. Human beings know the unavoidable certainty of death that everyone must face. All people must die once and after that face judgment. But Jesus has conquered death by rising from the dead. He has made it known that everyone who believes in him will be raised from the dead to live with him eternally. That is the language of faith in Christ.

- Does God answer prayers that are offered in faith? Does he listen to our prayers? Sometimes there is no answer and heaven appears to be closed. Although it seems that God has turned a deaf ear to us, he at times is trying our patience to strengthen our faith. Thus, Jesus told Jairus not to fear but to keep on believing.

- Throughout his ministry Jesus would repeatedly say to his disciples and others: "Fear not!" Fear drives away faith, but faith banishes fear. Scripture instructs us to keep our eye of faith fixed on Jesus, who is the author and perfecter of our faith.

- Jesus came to repair that which is broken by sin. The first Adam lived in a perfect world created by God, but his disobedience cast a long shadow over God's beautiful world. Death entered his creation and reigned supreme. The second Adam, Jesus, came to bring restoration and eventually an end to death. The resurrections of the daughter of Jairus, the young man of Nain, and Lazarus were early forerunners of the final resurrection at the end of time. Jesus died on the cross, rose from the dead to live eternally, and conquered death. Yet the power of death remains until the consummation. At that time bodies and souls shall be reunited in glory to live with Jesus on a renewed earth. That will be heaven on earth.

LAZARUS

John 11:1–44

Friends in Bethany

Two sisters, Mary and Martha, and their brother Lazarus lived in a house situated in the little village called Bethany about two miles to the east of Jerusalem. Apparently they were not the poorest in the land, for from time to time they entertained visitors and provided lodging for them in their spacious house. Jesus and his twelve disciples came to their home from time to time. Also some of the more prestigious Jews in the capital city were among their friends.

A relationship had developed between Jesus and his friends at Bethany that was much closer than casual familiarity. Cords of human love were strengthened during his frequent visits when he came to Jerusalem for stated festivals.

At one time Jesus and his disciples were staying on the east side of the Jordan, where they could be safe from potential harm by Jewish authorities. While he was there, Mary and Martha sent a messenger to Jesus with a short but urgent notice that said, "Lord, the one you love is sick." It implied that because Lazarus was ill and at the point of death, Jesus's help was urgently needed.

Instead of making haste to travel to Bethany and provide healing for his sick friend, Jesus stayed two more days before he responded to the call for help. He made it known to his disciples that the ailment of Lazarus was not life-threatening. He added that Lazarus's condition was to display God's glory so that the Son might be glorified through it.

Jesus's remark pointed to a miracle that would occur in Bethany so that the focus would not be on death but on the glory of God and his Son Jesus Christ. Jesus loved his friends Mary, Martha, and Lazarus; nevertheless, he waited two days before he responded to their request and began his trip to Judea.

Jesus told his disciples that Lazarus was asleep and that he would go to Bethany to wake him up. But if he dearly loved his friends, why did he delay his travels for two days? It had taken the messenger a day to come to Jesus; then there were two days of waiting, and last there was another day of travel for Jesus to come to his friends. By that time a total of four days had gone by. Why the delay?

Sorrowing Friends

The disciples understood Jesus to mean that natural sleep would restore Lazarus to health. But they should have realized that sleep for several days might not be understood literally. Jesus's reference to God's glory should have alerted them that something miraculous was going to happen.

Then Jesus told them plainly that his friend had died. And he added that he was glad not to have been at the house of his friend, so that his disciples might believe. With this remark he prepared them for the greatest miracle he would perform in the presence of all those who mourned the death of Lazarus in Bethany. He wanted them to see the power of God at work in raising a person who had died four days earlier.

The disciples had seen Jesus raise the young man of Nain and the daughter of Jairus, but these two had died only a short time before coming back to life. Now they followed Jesus on his way to Bethany, where they would meet the sorrowing Mary and Martha.

After a full day of traveling, Jesus and his disciples arrived at the home of the two sisters. With the women there were a number of Jews who had come from Jerusalem to comfort them. Martha heard about Jesus's arrival and came out to meet him, while her sister stayed inside with those who were consoling her.

Grief was written all over Martha's face, and the first words she spoke did not hide her disappointment: "Lord, if you had been here, my brother would not have died." All along the sisters had repeated these words, knowing that Jesus would have healed Lazarus if he had been there. But they also realized that Jesus would never have been able to arrive on time because their brother passed away soon after the messenger left. By now their brother had been in the tomb for four days.

Martha had steadfast faith in Jesus in spite of the death of her brother. She said to him, "But I know that whatever you ask of God, he will give it to you." When the messenger had returned to the sisters, he had related the words Jesus had spoken in response to the sisters' request to come. When Jesus heard the news about their brother's illness, he had said, "This illness will not cause death but is for the purpose of God's glory, so that the Son of God may be glorified through it." The sisters had heard this puzzling message and realized that Jesus had not forgotten their request. Thus Martha spoke words that expressed her unshaken faith in Jesus.

Answering Martha, Jesus reinforced her faith. He declared, "Your brother will rise again." Here was Jesus's explanation of his earlier remark that Lazarus's illness was not about death. She assumed that this remark was a reference to the resurrection from the dead. With confidence and assurance she answered, "I know that he will rise again in the resurrection on the last day." She expressed her firm belief that at the end of time the dead will be raised to a new life as the Old Testament teaches.

The possibility is not remote that Jesus had taught the doctrine of the resurrection at an earlier occasion in their home. Now he continued this teaching by saying to her: "I am the resurrection and the life; anyone who believes in me will live even though they die a natural death. And everyone who lives by believing in me will never die. Do you believe this?"

Jesus embodies the doctrines of the resurrection and of life with the bold words *I am.* As Jesus personifies these teachings, we must conclude that without him there is nothing except death. He teaches that both resurrection and life can be appropriated only by believing in him, that is, anyone who places faith in him rises from the dead and lives forever. This means that everyone who believes in Jesus on this side of the grave has already received the principle of life that can never be taken away.

Martha had heard Jesus teach these creeds in her home, and now in response to Jesus's question, she affirmed her faith in him. "Yes, Lord, I have believed; you are the Christ, the Son of God, coming into the world." As long as she kept her eye of faith fixed on Jesus she was spiritually secure. But the moment she looked away from him, doubt took over.

Then Martha went into the house to call Mary away from the people who were comforting her. She whispered to her that Jesus had arrived and said, "The Teacher is asking for you." She wanted the same privacy for Mary in the presence of Jesus that she herself had had. But it was all to no avail. The mourners inside the house saw Mary leave and assumed she was heading for the tomb to mourn there. So they followed her.

Mary came to Jesus, knelt at his feet, and spoke the same words Martha had uttered earlier: "Lord, if you had been here, my brother would not have died." When she burst into tears, Jesus was overcome with emotion and perturbed in spirit. He asked, "Where have you laid him?" Others answered the question for him by saying, "Lord, come and see."

The Miracle

Jesus approached the tomb where he witnessed the evidence of death's authority. He saw behind it the power of Satan, who had come to destroy and take away life—in this case the life of Lazarus. Jesus expressed his profound indignation toward Satan, the angel of death. He was deeply distressed in the presence of death.

"Jesus wept." These two words are known as the shortest verse in the New Testament. They speak volumes about his sympathy on the one hand and his anger against the angel of death on the other. Jesus expressed his sympathy to the grieving sisters and his outrage against the power of death. He quietly shed tears.

Prominent Jews who witnessed Jesus's reaction to the death of Lazarus were divided in their interpretation of what was taking place. Some were surprised at the expression of his love for the deceased, while others asked why he had not prevented Lazarus from dying. They knew that he had opened the eyes of a blind man, so they reasoned that Jesus should have displayed his authority in healing Lazarus.

The tomb had a stone laid across its entrance. When Jesus gave the order to remove it, Martha immediately reacted. She reminded him that Lazarus had been dead for four days—as if Jesus did not know. The penetrating smell of death hung over the entire area.

Jesus gently rebuked Martha for her lack of faith. He reminded her that if she believed, she would see the glory of God. These were the same words the messenger had conveyed to her when he returned from notifying Jesus. Jesus had told her that he personified the resurrection and the life. Martha had to acknowledge Jesus's words.

Strong men removed the stone. Then Jesus looked up to heaven and offered a prayer of thanks to God the Father in which he indicated that his request for the return of Lazarus had been granted. He did nothing on his own accord but always did everything in harmony with God's will. He uttered this audible prayer for the benefit of all those who heard him so that they might believe.

Jesus shouted three words in a loud voice, "Lazarus, come out!" Then the miracle happened. Lazarus came forth out of the tomb in full view of all who were present. He was able to walk with difficulty because his feet and his hands were tied with strips of linen, and he had a cloth over his face. We assume that his body had been covered with a burial sheet. Jesus told the bystanders to remove his grave clothes and let him go home, obviously to get dressed.

How did the miracle take place? We don't know apart from saying that it happened because God executed his will through Jesus's power. We would like to know how all the molecules came together in his body. We want to hear what Lazarus could tell his sisters and others about the life hereafter. But nothing is revealed. In fact, Paul relates that he was privileged to enter heaven but was not allowed to tell what he heard, for these words are too sacred to be told. Heaven is so different from earth that there is an inability to describe what the future is all about.

The Aftereffect

At this point in Jesus's ministry, the resurrection of Lazarus was indeed the greatest miracle he had performed. He did this so that those who were present at the tomb might witness and confess that God the Father had sent Jesus. When they in faith accepted this truth, they would know that he was their Messiah, the Son of God.

Many of the Jews who had come to comfort Mary put their faith in Jesus when they witnessed the miracle of raising Lazarus from the dead. They were the ones who went to the Pharisees with the news of the miracle Jesus had performed.

In reaction to hearing this news, the chief priests and Pharisees called a meeting of their government council to take action against Jesus. They saw him as a threat to their security in case there would be a massive uprising against Roman authority. Hence, they wanted to eliminate Jesus by force and said that it would be better for one man to die than for a nation to perish. Some time later the chief priests, revealing their hardened hearts, made plans to kill Lazarus, because they noticed that through his witness people put their faith in Jesus.

Points to Ponder

- Lazarus spent four days in heaven and returned to life on earth. Even though he had seen the glory of heaven, he once more had to live on earth. He again had to live a life stained by sin with the inevitable consequence of dying again at God's appointed time. Nonetheless, Lazarus, whose name means "God helps," was an eloquent witness for Christ and his kingdom.
- The soul and body of Lazarus were brought together when Jesus called him to come out of the tomb. By

contrast, on the day of resurrection his body will come forth in glorified form to be reunited with his glorious spirit. All believers will be glorified when Jesus returns. The graves will be opened, and all those who are alive at that moment will be transformed in the twinkling of an eye. And so we shall be with Jesus forever.

- Lazarus died and was raised to live on this earth until death would claim him once more. Jesus died and rose from the dead never to die again. While Lazarus remained a citizen of this earth, Jesus ascended bodily to heaven to take his place at the right hand of God.

- Sin is a blinding force that keeps people in the grip of Satan. All the evidence that God has made known cannot convince a sinner unless the miracle of regeneration takes place in his or her heart. It is by grace alone that we have been saved through faith. We can't claim credit, for it is a gift of God.

EYESIGHT RESTORED

Two Blind Men

Matthew 9:27–31

Lack of Sight

One of the five senses is sight. Although blindness is a bane, the other senses appear to fill in the lack of vision. The sense of hearing is sharper, and so are those of touch, smell, and taste. Nevertheless, the loss of eyesight remains a severe handicap.

In today's world, the blind receive help in their ability to read books by touch; they can find employment in many fields of labor; and they are afforded many conveniences to accommodate their needs. In Jesus's day the blind were relegated to the rank of beggars, which is still true today in underdeveloped countries. For them, the loss of eyesight means unavoidable poverty and an exclusive dependence on family members.

In some parts of the world, the causes of blindness are often due to neglect. Dust particles settle on the surface of the eyes, inflame them, and over time bring about partial or total loss of sight. Inflammation of the eyeballs when not treated medically and professionally may cause an inability to see. Also overexposure to the intense heat and brilliant light of the sun may eventually lead to blindness.

The Scriptures often speak about blindness. Isaac in his old age had impaired vision so that he could not distinguish the appearances of Jacob and Esau. In prison, Samson's eyes were put out by the Philistines to make him harmless. The prophet Elisha asked God to open the eyes of his enemies who were stricken with blindness when they entered the city of Samaria. Paul had poor eyesight and writes that the Galatians would have torn out their eyes and given them to him.

Blind Men

Jesus healed many people who were unable to see. Among them were two blind men who followed him and kept on calling out, "Have mercy on us, Son of David." They identified Jesus as the Son of David, which was equivalent to calling him Messiah. According to the prophecies in the Old Testament Scriptures, at his coming the Messiah would bring numerous blessings, among them the restoration of sight.

These two blind men followed Jesus, for they knew in their hearts that if Jesus was indeed the Messiah, he would grant them sight. Perhaps they had listened to him preach in his hometown synagogue of Nazareth. There he had said that in the year of the Lord he had come to preach good news to the poor, to proclaim freedom for the prisoners, and to give recovery of sight for the blind. Now they wanted to hear that Jesus was true to his word.

But the Teacher was not paying any attention to the two blind men. They continued their pleading to have mercy on them, to show them pity not merely in giving them alms but in granting them the gift of sight. As if he did not hear them, Jesus kept on walking toward the house where he was staying. By all appearances he showed callous indifference, but actually he was testing their faith. Although they acknowledged him as the Messiah, Jesus wanted to see if they really believed in him.

When they were inside the house, Jesus turned to them and asked if they believed that he was able to grant their request. The blind men were concise and to the point. They said, "Yes, Lord." That was sufficient for Jesus, who reached out to their eyes and touched them. He could also have spoken a single word, and they would have been healed. He did not make clay with his spittle and daub their eyes, nor did he put saliva on their eyes. But on this occasion the touch of the Master was sufficient.

Jesus said, "Because of your faith, let it be done to you." And at that moment the miracle happened. Jesus opened their eyes. We are not told about the joy and happiness of these two men. Understandably they were delighted to be able to see again. They no longer had to depend on family members for help. They no longer were beggars, for they now could find employment and earn a living.

When the men were ready to leave, Jesus gave them a stern warning not to tell anyone about the miracle. This order seems incongruous, for as soon as the men appeared in public they would be asked what had happened to them, and they would have to tell the people. The blind men did not receive sight out of nowhere; they had to relate what occurred and identify Jesus as the miracle-worker.

Jesus did not want the men to identify him as the Messiah because that would get him into trouble with the religious authorities and the members of the Jewish council. These people would not like to see him as one who could oppose Rome and thus cause an adverse reaction. Also the knowledge that he was indeed the Messiah would invite opposition to his ministry. Jesus allowed the formerly blind men to say that he healed them, but they were not to identify him as the Son of David, the Messiah.

However, the two men departed, and wherever they went they told the people what Jesus had done for them. As a result, the news of the miracle spread throughout the land. The last thing Jesus wanted was adverse publicity from those whom he had warned not to reveal his identity.

Points to Ponder

- Faith coupled with prayer restores a person who is ill or afflicted. The men put their faith in Jesus and petitioned him to have mercy. And on that basis he healed them. When in the wisdom of God no healing is granted, we should never blame the sick for lacking sufficient faith. If we do so, we place ourselves above God and thus commit a grievous sin.
- Jairus and his wife were told not to tell anyone that Jesus had raised their daughter. He did the same thing with the two men who had their sight restored. But these men deliberately disobeyed Jesus and spread the news throughout the land. Faith in Jesus and obedience to his precepts go hand in hand. Disobedience is a sin that undermines faith.
- The two men were blessed with spiritual insight when they addressed Jesus as the Son of David. Physical blindness need not be the same as spiritual blindness. In his grace and goodness God often gives spiritual sight to the physically handicapped.
- Physical sight is a treasure that God has given to us. But spiritual insight is a gift that is far greater because it relates to eternity. The people who are able to see spiritually know Jesus as their Savior, are filled with

love, express their thankfulness, and in word and deed serve him obediently whenever and wherever he sends them. They are his ambassadors who convey the good news of God's love and salvation to anyone willing to listen.

BARTIMAEUS

Matthew 20:29–34; Mark 10:46–52; Luke 18:35–43

Near Jericho

When the Israelites entered Canaan, God told them to destroy the city of Jericho. They did this by walking around it once a day for a week. Then on the seventh day they circled the city seven times, the priests blew their horns at the seventh time, and the walls of the city collapsed before their eyes. This was God's way of demolishing Jericho. He also gave the Israelites the warning never to rebuild the city, for anyone who would do so would pay the price of losing his firstborn son as well as his youngest son. This curse was fulfilled centuries later.

In later years King Herod the Great built a summer palace near old Jericho. Here the Roman administrative center was located and functioned as the new Jericho. Here the tax collectors working for the Romans lived in luxury. Between old and new Jericho, blind beggars sat asking the passing crowds to show pity by tossing them coins.

One of the beggars was named Bartimaeus, which meant "son of Timaeus." He and another beggar heard that Jesus was coming toward them. The name of Jesus of Nazareth was well-known to them because of the many miracles he had performed and the teaching he had done in countless places. So when Bartimaeus heard that Jesus was on his way to Jerusalem for the annual Passover Feast, he called out in a loud voice, "Jesus, Son of David, have mercy on me!"

Now that Jesus was passing by Jericho, Bartimaeus had a golden opportunity to beseech Jesus for the gift of sight. He would not stop calling out to him, even though the bystanders told the blind man to be quiet. Instead, the remarks of the crowd spurred him to even louder petitions.

Again and again Bartimaeus called on Jesus, the Son of David, to show him mercy. He acknowledged that this Jesus was indeed the Messiah promised in the Scriptures. He knew that this Messiah had the power to restore sight to the blind, as he had proven when he healed other blind people in both Galilee and Jerusalem. Certainly this man of God would not pass him by without granting him sight. Bartimaeus put his faith in Jesus, the Son of David.

A Conspicuous Miracle

Jesus heard the blind man's plea. It was obvious to him that the call for mercy did not mean giving the blind man a few coins but giving the two beggars the gift of sight. Jesus used the very bystanders who had rebuked the blind man to bring Bartimaeus and his blind companion to him. The onlookers did what the Master told them and said to Bartimaeus, "Cheer up, arise, he is calling you!"

Bartimaeus immediately responded by shaking off his cloak; he jumped up and went toward Jesus, most likely guided by people in the crowd. Jesus wanted the people to be involved in the miracle he was about to perform. He asked the blind man, "What do you want me to do for you?" The answer was moving, for Bartimaeus in his native tongue called him *Rabbouni,* which means "my great Teacher." Then he requested that he might see again.

Bartimaeus left his cloak and possibly some collected coins behind. He was not worried about a potential loss of his few possessions; he believed that regaining his sight was a gift that transcended all earthly goods. Sight would mean an end to living in darkness; it would mean seeing Jesus in person.

Jesus touched the eyes of the blind men. He did not put spittle or mud on their eyes; he did not utter an incantation; he did not use a charm. None of those accoutrements came into play. Then Bartimaeus heard Jesus say to him, "Go, your faith has healed you." Actually Jesus said by implication that his faith made him whole physically as well as spiritually. At that the two blind men were able to see again.

Yes, they could now see the blue sky, the green trees, and the red, white, and yellow flowers. Spiritually they knew that Jesus had healed them.

The joy, the happiness, the gratitude must have been over-whelming to the blind men who were now restored. They wanted to show their thankfulness to Jesus, and the most appropriate way to do so was to follow him as he was leaving Jericho on his way to Jerusalem. There Jesus would face the humiliation of the cross and death and also the exaltation of the resurrection from the dead. By faith the two men formerly blind but now seeing would experience the most important week in Jesus's earthly life.

Jesus did not stop Bartimaeus from addressing him with the messianic title *Son of David.* Days later when Jesus approached the city of Jerusalem, the crowds in front of him and those following him shouted, "Hosanna to the Son of David! Blessed is he who comes in the name of the Lord!" And when he entered the temple area, the children were shouting, "Hosanna to the Son of David!" Jesus was now known by this messianic title.

Points to Ponder

- Jesus invites sinners to call on his name and to ask for mercy. He not only hears our imperfect prayers hampered by formalism, routine, and selfishness, but he perfects our deficient petitions and then presents them to God the Father. That is, Jesus is our helper in the prayers we address to God in his name. He is our intercessor.

- Sin blinds us so that we fail to see God's guiding hand in our lives. When we come to our senses and ask him to open our spiritual eyes, we can see his hand leading and directing us to glorify his name. When we receive spiritual sight, we stand amazed at his mercy, love, and grace toward us.

- When God gives us the gift of spiritual insight, we can live a life of prudent foresight to his glory. Then we are able to lead and direct others so that they too may walk not in darkness but in the beauty of spiritual light. Together we may rejoice in the glorious truth God makes known to us in his Word.

BLIND MAN IN BETHSAIDA

Mark 8:22–26

A Place of Unbelief

Located along the northeastern shore of the Lake of Galilee and on the east side of the River Jordan, Bethsaida was home to some of Jesus's disciples—Peter, Andrew, and Philip. They were fishermen who lived up to the name of their town, Bethsaida, which means "house or place of fishing." In time, the place expanded from a village to a city that eventually became a capital. Nonetheless, in popular speech the citizenry continued to call it a village.

Jesus had performed many miracles in the towns of Chorazin, Capernaum, and Bethsaida. But when he saw no spiritual growth, he reproached these places by saying that it would be more bearable on the day of judgment for Sodom and Gomorrah than for them. He said that if the people of those two cities had seen the miracles he had performed in these three Galilean towns, they would have repented without delay. However, in spite of all the miracles he had performed, Jesus failed to see faith in Chorazin, Capernaum, and Bethsaida.

Within a short distance from Bethsaida, a large crowd of five thousand men had listened to Jesus's teaching. Then late in the afternoon of that day, Jesus had miraculously fed this immense crowd by breaking five bread cakes and two fishes. That news had spread to the citizens of Bethsaida.

One of the residents of Bethsaida was a blind man. At one time he had been able to see, but because of disease, accident, or neglect, he had lost his eyesight. Now he stumbled around in darkness, had to be led by family members and friends, and was consigned to living the life of a beggar.

Some of the people had taken the blind man by the hand, perhaps persuading him to go to Jesus. There may have been reluctance on his part to ask for healing, because it was not the blind man but those who brought him who asked Jesus to touch and heal him. Instead of merely speaking a word and restoring his sight, Jesus took the blind man by the hand. He led him away from Bethsaida to a quiet place for the sake of privacy.

A Two-Stage Miracle

Jesus showed tender loving care by personally leading the blind man by the hand, undoubtedly talking to him and becoming acquainted with him. At a quiet place, he stopped and then spat on the man's eyes. Spittle was commonly believed to have medicinal value in healing blindness. Jesus chose this method to lead the blind man in stages to a firm faith in him. Next, he tenderly put his hands on him and asked if he could see anything. The man looked up and replied that he could see people walking around who looked like trees to him. He remembered the sizes and shapes of trees from the time he still had sight. He was looking at Jesus's disciples and noticed that they were moving objects. The images he saw were indistinct and blurred. He had to be personally involved and come

179

to the realization that the healing process was only half complete.

Then Jesus followed through with the second stage. He once more laid his hands on the man by touching his eyes. When the man opened his eyelids wide and focused intently, he could see everything plainly. The man's sight was put right in two stages that lasted only a fraction of time. The first person he looked at was Jesus, his benefactor. After that he looked around to see objects near and far, to admire the colors in nature, and to connect familiar voices with faces. His eyesight was completely restored.

It was now time for the man to go home, but Jesus gave him strict instruction not to go back into the village. This should not be understood that the man could not go to his house. It probably meant that he should not continue his status as a beggar. As a useful citizen, he could now be gainfully employed and hold an honorable position in society.

Points to Ponder

- By reading Scripture we are able to see spiritual truths, which the Holy Spirit makes us see ever more clearly by opening our spiritual eyes. The nineteenth-century hymn writer Clara H. Scott put it eloquently in the following lines:

  Open my eyes, that I may see
  Glimpses of truth Thou hast for me;
  Place in my hands the wonderful key
  That shall unclasp and set me free.

  Silently now I wait for Thee,
  Ready my God, Thy will to see,
  Open my eyes, Illumine me,
  Spirit Divine!

- As the blind man's eyes were opened so that he could look into Jesus's face, so we as believers will be given the joyful experience of seeing Jesus when we leave this earthly scene and enter the portals of heaven.
- People who are able to see spiritually are filled with wisdom that God gives them in answer to prayer. With this gift of wisdom they give leadership in their family, at church, at work, and in society. This heavenly gift is a treasure that keeps them on the right road that yields a harvest of righteousness.

THE MAN BORN BLIND

John 9:1–41

Healing Ministry

To be born blind means that one has never seen any light at all. It connotes living in a world totally devoid of color, beauty, and splendor. For the blind, it is an impenetrably dark existence in which one moves about by relying on the senses of touch, smell, taste, and hearing.

Jesus and his disciples were walking in Jerusalem perhaps near the temple where beggars were accustomed to sit. They saw a well-known beggar who had been blind since birth. His blindness may have been caused by a lingering effect of venereal disease. Scripture merely states the fact that the man was blind without providing an explanation about a possible cause.

The disciples asked Jesus whether this blindness was the result of the man's sin or that of his parents. Like the Jewish leaders of that day, they considered all suffering a result of sin. But how could a baby commit sin before it was born? Were the disciples thinking of the twin babies Jacob and

Esau, who were struggling in the womb? Perhaps, but what would the sin of the parents have been?

Jesus told them pointedly that sin was not the issue. Instead he called attention to the works that God would display in the man. That is, Jesus looked at the blind beggar and asked what he could do for him. The disciples, by contrast, saw the man and questioned what the cause of the man's blindness might have been. In short, Jesus looked forward while his disciples looked backward.

When Jesus referred to the works of God, he insinuated that a miraculous healing was about to occur. This action would demonstrate God's glory. That is, the blind man would be able to see physically but also spiritually, and that would be a double miracle. This was the work of God the Father and of God the Son. To put it differently, God worked through his Son Jesus Christ, who was his agent, the one who was sent. Jesus identified himself as the light of the world.

In the case of the deaf and mute man in the Decapolis, Jesus moistened his fingertips with saliva and then touched the man's tongue. And when he healed the blind man at Bethsaida, he put spittle on the man's eyes. This time Jesus spat on the ground and with the dirt made moist clay, which he daubed on the eyelids of the blind man.

Some in Jesus's day would have seen this as a medicinal use of saliva. However, it is better to say that Jesus put mud on the eyelids of the man to make him even blinder than he already was. The man had to be personally involved by showing his willingness to do what Jesus told him. No doubt he had heard Jesus teach in Solomon's Colonnade in the temple area as he sat there begging. Now he had to act in obedience on faith in the one whom God had sent. Then he would be healed by obeying the miracle-worker. When Jesus told the blind man to go to the Pool of Siloam and wash his eyes, he was testing him to see whether he would put his trust in Jesus.

The man knew exactly where the Pool of Siloam was located—inside the city wall in the southeast corner of Jerusalem. Many centuries earlier King Hezekiah had constructed a tunnel to convey water from the Spring Gihon to the Pool of Siloam so that in time of siege the city would always have a ready supply of water available.

Perhaps guided by a friend, the blind man went to the pool and washed away the dirt from his eyelids. Then he opened his eyes and was delighted to see the blue sky, the fluffy white clouds, the green grass and trees, and the color of flowers, water, and the stone walls. He now was able to put sounds and sight together, and he recognized the people around him. He did not need anyone to guide him, for he now could see. He rushed home to see his father and mother and tell them the news of the miracle that had occurred.

Controversy

When the man came into his own neighborhood, people were confused. Some said that he was indeed the blind man, but others thought a look-alike had come to their area. Then the man identified himself and said that he indeed was the beggar. As soon as he made this known, he had to explain to the people how it was that he now was able to see.

The man told his neighbors in plain words that Jesus had spat on the ground and had made mud. Then he had put the mud on his eyes and instructed him to go to the Pool of Siloam and wash away the dirt. When the blind man had done that, he was able to open his eyes and see.

The people brought the man to the religious authorities to get answers to this occurrence. They wanted to know what their leaders thought about the marvel of granting sight to a man born blind. The Pharisees turned to the formerly blind man for an explanation. He told them the same story he had given his neighbors.

The strict Sabbath-keeping Pharisees, however, reacted not with joy but with anger because work had been involved in healing this man on the day of rest. They said that it was impossible for Jesus to be a man of God because he had desecrated the Sabbath by performing work. In their interpretation Jesus had committed a threefold sin:

- making mud,
- applying it, and
- healing the man.

Others reacted favorably to what had occurred. They reasoned that a sinner would not be capable of executing miracles, but Jesus had performed a miracle and thus proved beyond a shadow of a doubt that God was with him and had commissioned him to be his messenger.

On the basis of the evidence, one would think the Pharisees would have to admit that Jesus indeed was sent by God. They would have to acknowledge that Jesus had healed a congenital blindness, which in all of Israel's history had never happened. They would have to concede that giving sight to the blind was an act of God and not of Satan. Only God could give Jesus the authority to heal the blind man. But this fact they adamantly refused to admit.

Instead, the Pharisees called for a formal meeting to investigate the matter. The irony was that by calling an investigation on the Sabbath to charge Jesus with desecrating the day of rest, they themselves became guilty as well. They conveniently ignored the Sabbath rules as they applied to themselves because they considered it of utmost importance to discredit Jesus. They had made it known that anyone who confessed him as the Christ would be expelled from the local synagogue.

The religious leaders considered the erstwhile blind man their first witness in the case, and they regarded him as one of Jesus's followers. They wanted to know what the man would say about his benefactor. The former beggar was sagacious and prudent and merely answered their questions in straightforward terms. He simply replied, "He is a prophet." But this answer did not satisfy them.

The Pharisees called in the parents of the man as their next witnesses. They expected the parents to be forthright in giving answers to their pointed questions. They wanted to know if the man was their son and whether he was born blind. The parents could testify that this was indeed the case. Then they were asked how he had received his sight. The implicit answer to this question had to involve the person and name of Jesus.

The parents knew that if they openly stated the fact that Jesus had opened their son's eyes, they would be excommunicated. They knew the stipulation of the Pharisees. Anyone who acknowledged that Jesus was the Christ would be forced out of the local synagogue. So the parents took the safe route by pleading ignorance and placing the burden of proof on the shoulders of their son. Their answer to the religious leaders was that they should ask him, for he was of age.

The Trial

The parents tried to play it safe by being noncommittal, but by contrast the son was not afraid. He had been blessed with a keen mind and a retentive memory. While sitting as a beggar near the temple on a daily basis, he had heard the debates of the Pharisees and the teachers of the Law. They recited portions of the Scriptures and by means of questions and answers discussed the meaning of certain words and passages. The blind man had absorbed these readings from God's Word and the theological dialogues and had stored them in his memory. He had also mentally sharpened his debating skills.

186

When the former beggar was called before the meeting a second time, he was not at all fearful. He was ready to meet the challenge of facing the clergy and debating them on their own turf.

The interrogators said to him, "Give glory to God!" This is the same as saying to a present-day witness to "tell the truth, the whole truth, and nothing but the truth!" They were certain that the man had not told them the truth when he stated that Jesus was a prophet. They wanted to hear him denounce Jesus as the Messiah. That, in their opinion, was telling the truth.

The Pharisees said, "We know that this man is a sinner." They were referring to Jesus, who broke the Sabbath commandment by making mud and healing the blind man. The man's approach in replying to their statement was sagacious. He avoided getting entangled in judging Jesus as a sinner. His answer was both negative and positive: "Whether Jesus is a sinner or not, I do not know. One thing I do know: I was blind, but now I see." He put off giving further information.

They tried to have him repeat all the details concerning the healing miracle. They inquired, "What did he do to you? How did he open your eyes?" The man realized that they were going over the same territory twice, and he refused to be part of it. He confronted them and, unafraid, called their bluff by telling them that they already knew the information. He wanted to know why they were asking questions to which they already knew the answers. Then he boldly asked them if they wanted to become disciples of Jesus too.

Of course the Pharisees were not interested in becoming Jesus's disciples. And certainly they did not want to hear it from a low-class beggar. They hurled invectives at the man and tried to humiliate him. They described themselves as disciples of Moses, while they looked down on the man for being a follower of Jesus. They went so far as to say that they did not even know where Jesus came from. This meant that they knew and obeyed the Law of Moses, but Jesus, whom they disparagingly called "this fellow," had no credentials.

Relying on his knowledge of the Scriptures, the former beggar said: "Now that's remarkable! You don't know where he comes from, and yet he opened my eyes!" He hinted at prophecies of the prophet Isaiah, who at various places in his book had spoken about restoration of sight in the messianic age. The fact that Jesus opened the man's eyes therefore pointed to his messiahship.

Then the man continued and clarified the identity of Jesus, which he had put off earlier. He candidly said, "We know that God does not listen to sinners, but he listens to anyone who is devout and does his will." That was an irrefutable statement, and the man's logic was sound. He continued and stated, "Since the beginning of time, it has never been heard that someone has opened the eyes of one born blind." The former beggar took a backseat to no one and proved that he knew the history of his people. The healing of a man born blind was unique and without parallel. Then he said, "If this man were not from God, he would not be able to do anything." The man used indisputable logic to make his point. He rested his case.

The negative reaction from the Pharisees was predictable but below par. Instead of admitting their defeat, they demeaned their opponent by saying that he was born in sin. They said that sin was the cause of his congenital blindness. Then they expelled him from the synagogue.

A Second Miracle

After Jesus performed the miracle of opening the man's physical eyes, he later returned to him to perform the miracle of opening his spiritual eyes. He heard that the Pharisees had excommunicated the man. Cut off from Jewish society, the former beggar had nowhere to go. But Jesus found him and asked if he believed in the Son of Man. That is, Jesus wanted to know whether he believed, in contrast to the Pharisees who refused to believe.

While the man was blind he had heard the voice of Jesus but had not seen him. Now he put voice and face together and cautiously asked, "Who is he, sir? Tell me that I may believe in him."

Jesus identified himself as the Son of Man, namely, the Son of God. He told him that he was the one speaking to him. At an earlier occasion a Samaritan woman wanted to know whether Jesus was the Messiah, and he had spoken the same words: "The one speaking to you is he."

The man then acknowledged his faith in Jesus and worshiped him. The miracle of conversion had taken place.

Points to Ponder

- At times suffering is the result of sin, as in the case of abuse to the physical body. But we cannot say that all suffering is the result of sin. This is what the friends of Job tried to tell him, but God was angry with them. Job had to pray for them that God would not deal with them according to their folly. And God listened to him.
- The man who received the gift of sight was not spiritually blind, but the Pharisees lacked spiritual vision and were unable to see Jesus as the Messiah. Often in heated debates, some people refuse to see the broader picture and focus instead on minor details. But in this case, the leaders in Israel were spiritually blind by choice and refused to admit it.
- The person who defends the truth, promotes honesty, and champions the cause of justice is often vilified. The arrows of the evil one are aimed at the righteous. Paul tells us to shield ourselves against Satan's fiery darts by

means of the shield of faith and to hold in our hand the sword of the Spirit, which is the Word of God.

- There are instances when parents cut off a son or daughter who has become a believer in Jesus. Where should this person go for comfort? Scripture is the primary source to find consolation. For instance, in time of need I recommend that you read the Psalms that teach, "Father and mother may forsake you, but the LORD will look after you."

LEPERS CLEANSED

THE CLEANSING OF A LEPER

Matthew 8:1–4; Mark 1:40–45; Luke 5:12–16

From Top to Bottom

In ancient times, leprosy was the worst sickness among all physical diseases. As the most fearful of all illnesses, it could be called a living death. Gradually and slowly, one's physical body degenerated; the face and extremities of the body were severely affected, decomposed, and fell away. Eventually hands were without fingers, feet without toes, and heads with deformed eyebrows, eyelids, nose, lips, and ears. Nerve endings no longer registered pain, so a patient was not fully aware of the body's gradual destruction. In advanced cases, gangrene caused parts of the body to become misshapen and die. As a result, an unpleasant odor surrounded the unfortunate individual.

As a rule, anyone with leprosy was banned from society and forced to live in a colony of lepers. Nearby relatives and friends brought food, beverages, and other necessities to sustain the lepers. The sufferers in the colony would pine away until death released them from their misery.

An exception was Naaman, the Syrian general. He traveled to Israel accompanied by his servants and arrived at Samaria, where the prophet Elisha told him to wash himself seven times in the River Jordan. He obeyed, and his body was restored.

Until the middle of the twentieth century, physicians had no way to counteract this incurable disease. Leprosy, now known as Hansen's disease, is a malady that turns the skin white. Bacteria multiply ceaselessly and affect a person's skin, nerves, and membranes.

Modern medicine has made large strides in limiting the spread of the disease, which had been especially widespread in tropical and subtropical regions of the world. Patients can now be treated with antibiotics. Nonetheless, those parts of the body that have been affected can never be restored.

During Jesus's ministry, he healed lepers and brought back the body parts that had been affected or even lost. As he was traveling through one of the cities, a certain leper approached him and knelt before him. This leper was in an advanced stage of the disease, for all his body parts were affected. He was a pitiful sight so that people rushed away from him for fear of contamination. They did not want to view his horrible appearance. The leper was kept inside a colony, and if he was away from it, he had to shout, "Unclean, unclean."

The leper was a man of unwavering faith; he was determined to see the great miracle-worker. Although everyone had fled, Jesus stood quietly waiting for the man to approach him. The leper's earnest request was to be healed by Jesus, if he was willing. He had probably heard from other people who had been healed that the Great Physician was able to cure him. He dropped to his knees with his face to the ground and humbly implored Jesus to help him.

This was the profound worship of a stricken individual who honored Christ by addressing him as Lord. He politely asked Jesus if he was willing to heal him, put himself at his mercy, and awaited his willingness.

Filled with compassion, Jesus reached out to the hapless man and touched him. Those who watched Jesus touch the leper must have thought his action was unsafe and unwise and would have perilous consequences. However, Jesus, who was pure, touched the impure without contracting impurities. Because of his divine power, Jesus was impervious to the disease. He spoke the words, "I will, be cleansed," and his purity entered the leper, who immediately was cleansed and completely healed. Note that the impurity of the leper did not enter Jesus, but his purity entered and healed the man.

The leper looked at his hands and feet and saw that all his fingers and toes had reappeared in perfect shape. He touched his face and felt his eyebrows, eyelashes, ears, lips, and nose; he realized that all the parts of his body were back to normal. He again had the sense of feeling, and his skin once again had a normal, healthy color. He had asked for purification and had received restoration. His joy and happiness knew no end.

Timely Instructions

By restoring the man to perfect health, Jesus had given him renewed access to society, synagogue, and temple. But before the man could rush to see his family and friends and tell them about the miracle, he first had to go to the priest in Jerusalem. There the priest had to examine him and declare him healed. Afterward he would have to bring an offering in accordance with the Law of Moses.

At the temple, the clergy would ask the man how he was healed of leprosy. He would have to tell them that Jesus of Nazareth had healed him with a mere touch of his hand and an authoritative command. The priests would have to acknowledge Jesus's power to heal leprous people, including a man who once was covered with the disease. They were unable to refute the evidence that came to them in the person of this former leper. While Jesus had restored him to health and happiness, the priests had no such ability and could only declare him healed.

Jesus had instructed the man to go directly to Jerusalem and offer a gift prescribed in the Mosaic Law. This act served as a testimony to the priests, who were forced to concede that Christ was indeed sent by God. Thus, the offering of the man was not a sin offering but rather a witness to Jesus, who had come not to destroy the law but to fulfill it.

Jesus's instructions included a prohibition not to tell anyone. He sternly charged the healed man to keep quiet. He wanted to avoid, first, an untimely conflict with the religious establishment in Jerusalem and, next, a misunderstanding of the people who saw him only as a miracle-worker instead of God's messenger sent to save them.

The news spread like wildfire and could not be stopped, and great multitudes came to Jesus as a result. People came to listen to him and to be healed from their afflictions. But the end result was that Jesus had to withdraw himself to lonely places where he had time to rest and pray.

Points to Ponder

- The difference between Jesus and a faith healer is telling. Jesus healed the people instantly. A paralytic stood up and walked; dead people came back to life; a leper was completely restored with all his body parts intact. No faith healer is able to do anything similar to the miracles Jesus performed.
- The miracles Jesus performed were in support of his teaching. The common people perceived his divine authority and saw that his message differed from that

196

of the scribes and Pharisees. In the days of Jesus and the apostles, God accompanied the teaching of his Word with signs and wonders. When the apostolic era ended, the extraordinary miracles ceased.

- The touch of Jesus's hand extended to the sick reveals his deep compassion and love. Similarly, a word of comfort from us accompanied by a mere touch expresses our Christian love to those who are hurting and suffering.

- Showing compassion and love to people in need is one of the hallmarks of Christianity. The apostle Paul writes that we should express loving care to all people, and especially to the members of the Christian church. Mercy and grace are God's characteristics that should be exemplified in his people and extended to those who are poor in this world.

TEN LEPERS HEALED

Luke 17:11–19

Jews and Samaritans

The discord between Jews and Samaritans was somewhat like the conflict between Jews and Palestinians today. Two nations live next to one another, but conflicts keep them separate.

The history of the Samaritans goes back to the time when the ten tribes were exiled. After the Jews were deported, the Assyrians brought in colonists from other nations. They appointed a Jewish priest to teach these settlers how to worship God. The settlers, called Samaritans, had the Scriptures of only the five books of Moses and nothing more. In later times when the Jews returned from exile to rebuild Jerusalem and the temple, they rebuffed the Samaritans who offered their help.

Throughout the centuries the relations between Jews and Samaritans were not the best. Galilean Jews would bypass Samaria, cross the Jordan, and travel on the east side of the river toward Judea. However, from time to time Jesus reached out to the Samaritans by traveling through their territory and showing kindness to individual inhabitants:

- He conversed with the Samaritan woman at the well, who rushed into the city of Sychar to tell the people about Jesus the Messiah.
- He told the parable of the Good Samaritan as a lesson to a Jewish teacher of the Law who had a narrow view of the concept *neighbor*.
- He rebuked his disciples John and James when they wanted him to call down fire from heaven to destroy a Samaritan village.

On his way to Jerusalem, Jesus and his disciples were at the border between Samaria and Galilee. They were traveling in an easterly direction with Samaria on the right and Galilee on the left. Their plan was to cross the Jordan and head south toward Jericho, where they would have to traverse the river once more.

Along the border of these two regions, Jesus entered a village and saw on its outskirts in the distance a group of ten lepers living together in a colony. Because of their illness, they had to live in solitary quarters and were not allowed to come near anyone. As patients suffering of the same disease, national differences were put aside. That is, the colony housed Jews as well as Samaritans, who in isolation sought and needed each other's company. Both the Jewish and the Samaritan lepers faced a slow but certain death. They had no other choice than to help one another.

They had heard about the healing ministry of Jesus, and when they saw him traveling, although removed from them by a distance, they took the opportunity to call out in a loud voice: "Jesus, Master, have mercy on us!" The law forbade them to approach Jesus, so they had to resort to shouting. Their cry for mercy conveyed a plea for Jesus to heal them.

They did not have to be specific, for their condition in isolation was sufficiently clear. They wanted to be healed.

Gratitude and Indifference

Leprosy is a disease that affects a patient's vocal cords to the point of becoming voiceless. However, some of the sufferers who called on Jesus were able to shout loud enough for him to hear their plea for help.

Whereas on an earlier occasion Jesus had touched a leper, this time he stayed away with his disciples. Jesus called out to the ten lepers, "Go and show yourselves to the priests." He said nothing about faith, yet the fact that they were told to start traveling without being healed demanded trust on their part. He merely said that they should show themselves to the religious authorities to be declared cleansed, even though they were still covered with leprosy.

When they began walking away from the camp, they suddenly realized that Jesus had healed them. They looked at their hands, their feet, and each other's faces. Then they saw that their bodies were completely restored to normalcy. Perhaps at that moment national pride took hold. The Jews wanted to hasten to the priests but not in the company of a Samaritan. They said that he ought to go to his own priest.

The Samaritan, however, saw that his body was completely healed. His vocal cords were restored, and he shouted for joy. He stopped in his tracks, turned around, and walked toward Jesus. His heart was filled with gratitude. Instead of facing a slow and certain death, he now had a new life ahead of him. He fell on his face at the feet of Jesus to pay homage and express his sincere gratitude to his benefactor.

Here was a Samaritan who thanked a Jew for the gift of health restored. But he was the one and only out of a group of ten lepers who all were healed. The other nine were on their way to the priests and never turned around to thank Jesus.

Jesus had noticed the nationalistic traits of the nine Jews who now no longer had fellowship with the despised Samaritan. He asked three questions: "Were there not ten who were healed? Where are the nine? Were none found to return and give praise to God, except this foreigner?"

Ten lepers had expressed their desire to be healed. Audibly and inaudibly they had voiced the plea,

> Lord, have mercy;
>   Christ, have mercy;
>   Lord, have mercy on us.

Jesus had responded to their petition by healing all of them. All the lepers were healed, but only one returned to give thanks. He prostrated himself in front of Jesus, who told him to stand up because his faith had saved him. The Samaritan received a double blessing: being healed physically and being saved spiritually. He now became a disciple of Jesus, eternally thankful for his salvation.

The faith of the nine Jews was superficial and vanished once they were healed. They had faith in miracles but only momentarily. They were ungrateful and at the same time unwilling to risk becoming followers of Jesus. And last, they used Jesus for their own physical interests and after that had no further need of him.

Ingratitude to God ultimately leads to rejecting him, and rejecting him ends in falling away from God. The writer of the letter to the Hebrews expresses himself in these words: "Let us give thanks, and so worship God acceptably with holy fear and awe, for our God is a consuming fire."

The Samaritan went on his way living a life of gratitude by telling others about Jesus. Thankfulness always has the result that God adds abundant blessings to those who love him and do his will. They are happy and joyful people, partakers of life's riches, materially and spiritually.

Points to Ponder

- The rules of common courtesy impel us to thank others for gifts we receive from them. We express our thanks verbally or by sending a thank-you note. Negligence to express thanks is never appreciated. It is considered discourteous and rude.
- Gifts from God come in the form of food and drink, three meals a day, clothing, housing, transportation, recreation, work, friends, health, finances, freedom, and numerous spiritual blessings. God's people ought to thank him daily and repeatedly for all the benefits they receive. I suggest that you adopt the rule to begin each day in prayer and end each day with thanksgiving.
- God always rejoices when his people utter expressions of gratitude. Whenever they thank him, they glorify his name. By thanking and glorifying him, they fulfill the first petition of the Lord's Prayer, "Hallowed be your name."
- National and linguistic barriers often stand in the way of expressing our love to other people. Especially when certain nations have fought each other at war and hurtful feelings are evident, the people involved may find Jesus's command to love their neighbor almost impossible. Jesus set the example by healing both Jews and a Samaritan, and only the latter showed gratitude toward him.

LAME WALK AGAIN

THE HEALING OF A PARALYTIC

Matthew 9:2–8; Mark 2:1–12; Luke 5:18–26

At Home in Capernaum

Jesus regularly roamed the countryside teaching the people and healing the sick. But there were also times when he stayed at home in Capernaum, which had become his adopted town. He may have taken up residence in the home of Simon Peter, the spokesman of his disciples. This house probably was quite spacious and could accommodate a sizable group of people who had come to listen to Jesus.

On one occasion, Pharisees and learned teachers of the Law who resided in many villages of Galilee and Judea and in Jerusalem had come to the house where Jesus was teaching. These members of the clergy had not come to welcome the Teacher as one of them. On the contrary, they were there to find out whether his teaching was mainstream doctrine in harmony with theirs. If there was any deviation from the tenets they held and taught, they would promptly report it to the authorities in Jerusalem.

Jesus's listeners had to admit that he was endowed with supernatural power to heal the sick. That power could only be attributed to God, who had sent Jesus to do his work. The clergy might be skeptical about his teaching, but they had to admit that the reports they had heard about sick people restored to normal health were indeed noteworthy. Jesus was a miracle-worker in the likeness of Elijah and Elisha. Honesty would compel them to accept him not merely as a prophet but as the Messiah, the Son of God.

Remarkable Faith

One of the citizens in Capernaum was paralyzed from the neck down, probably because of an accident. He was confined to his cot and needed daily care provided by his family members. He had heard about the miracles Jesus had performed among some people in his town, including the servant of a Roman centurion, Peter's mother-in-law, and a demon-possessed man.

The paralytic wondered whether Jesus would be willing to heal him too. He discussed his desire to be healed with four friends, who immediately agreed that Jesus indeed could make him well. His friends each took a corner of his mat, picked him up, and carried him toward the house where Jesus was.

When they came to the house, a crowd blocked the entrance, making it impossible for them to see Jesus. They could hear his voice but were unable to come near him. Nothing could stop these determined men. They noticed the outside staircase on the side of the house that led to a flat roof made of hardened dirt. Resourcefully they carried the man to the spot where they could hear, down below, Jesus teaching the people. They started digging through the roof. When the hole was big enough, they let down the man on his mat right in front of Jesus.

As could be expected, the audience was more interested in what was happening to the ceiling than in listening to Jesus. All eyes were fixed on the paralyzed man being lowered by his four friends. What would Jesus do? To say the least, this was a rude intrusion and an unusual interruption. But the Teacher was not at all perturbed.

Jesus saw the faith of the men who ingeniously had lowered the paralytic right in front of him. He addressed the paralytic and said, "Take heart, son, your sins are forgiven." No scolding came from his lips but instead a word of encouragement. His tone of voice indicated that he would take care of both his soul and body.

But the teachers of the Law and the Pharisees were not at all pleased with Jesus' statement about forgiving sins. Only God could forgive sins, not a mere mortal man. Who did Jesus think he was?

Jesus, the Son of God

Jesus faced the grumbling clergy head-on with an object lesson regarding his identity. He dealt first with the man's soul and then with his body. He told the paralytic to be of good cheer, because he knew the man's heart and saw his faith to be healed. He did not say anything about a relation between sin and paralysis. Jesus took care of the man's soul by declaring his sins forgiven. He knew that the Pharisees and teachers of the Law would voice their objections. But Jesus wanted them to know that he, as God's Son, had authority to forgive sins. He would prove this by healing the body of the paralyzed man.

The teachers of the Law mumbled in their beards that this fellow, speaking words of blasphemy, put himself on the level of God by forgiving a man's sins. They referred to Jesus not by name but with a contemptuous slur, "this fellow." In their minds, Jesus had committed blasphemy. And blasphemy had to be punished with the death penalty.

Jesus knew exactly what was going on in their hearts. With a twofold question he put to them a dilemma: "Which is easier, to say to a paralytic, your sins are forgiven, or to say to him, arise, take your mat, and walk?" Obviously, no one but God could forgive the man's sins, and no one but God could heal the paralytic and enable him to walk. Jesus put the emphasis on the verb *to say*, not on doing something extraordinary.

Then Jesus added, "That you may know that the Son of Man has authority to forgive sins on the earth." With the title *Son of Man* he clearly identified himself. The teachers of the Law immediately thought of the Old Testament Scripture that revealed a son of man to whom God had given authority, glory, and sovereign power. They knew that this person was the Messiah. However, Jesus was not any son of man, but he was the one and only Son of Man. This title was the equivalent of *Son of God*.

If then Jesus as the Son of Man had authority, he could perform the miracle of healing the paralytic's body. He exercised that power by telling the man to arise, take up his mat, and go home.

In front of the astonished bystanders, the man did exactly that. He got up, rolled up his mat, and departed. Jesus proved his identity by performing a supernatural miracle of instantaneously healing a paralytic. He proved that he could both forgive sins and heal the sick.

The man did not forget to give thanks. He went home glorifying God and praising his name. Similarly, the onlookers were filled with awe and glorified God. They were amazed and talked to one another about having seen incredible things. They had seen Jesus's power in both a spiritual and a physical dimension. He truly showed himself to be the Redeemer of body and soul.

Points to Ponder

- In 1563 a document was published in Heidelberg, Germany, which bears the name of its city: The Heidelberg Catechism. It consists of 129 questions and answers about the Christian religion. The first question is, "What is your only comfort in life and death?" The basic answer is, "That I am not my own, but belong—body and soul, in life and in death—to my faithful Savior Jesus Christ."

- The teachers of the Law and the Pharisees could not see the forest because of the trees. They observed the Ten Commandments and had added more than six hundred man-made regulations. But their religious shortsightedness prevented them from seeing their long-awaited Messiah, who was standing in their midst. They should have been among the first to welcome him as Lord and Savior.

- Active faith demands hard work physically and spiritually. I propose the timeworn motto: "Pray as if everything depends on God, and work as if everything depends on you!" We must daily pray and work for God's greater glory.

- The combined faith of five men brought about complete restoration to one of them. Jesus saw their faith and healed the paralytic. When determined people come together in prayer and ask God to bless their efforts that affect his church and kingdom, miracles happen. He opens the windows of heaven and pours out his blessings on those who wait for him in faith and prayer. He is always true to his Word and keeps his promises.

MAN AT THE POOL OF BETHESDA

John 5:1–15

Paralyzed for Thirty-Eight Years

The name *Bethesda* in Aramaic means "house of mercy." It is an apt description of a pool of mineral water in which the sick found relief and at times healing. The water had curative properties in healing various diseases. Numerous sick people came to the pool, including the blind, the crippled, and the paralytics.

Bethesda was a place marked by five covered colonnades. It was a well-known site for those who sought healing. Of course, it remained a question whether they found a cure or not. From time to time internal pressure caused the water to be agitated. People commonly believed that an angel caused the stir. Supposedly the first patient entering the pool would be healed.

The pool was near the Sheep Gate in the northeast corner of Jerusalem. Many sick folk sat or lay down near the edge of the pool in the shade of the five covered porches.

One of the men at the pool had been ill for thirty-eight years. Some people called him a paralytic, but in earlier years he might have been just crippled. In the course of time his condition had worsened, he had lost weight, and he was mentally despondent. Family members or friends had to carry him to and from the pool and had to tend to his daily needs.

The mineral water of the pool had not done the paralytic any good. Although some people might have experienced healing, many patients could testify that Bethesda was not so much a house of mercy as a house of misery. This sufferer had lost all hope of being healed.

Jesus walked up to the man and asked him how long he had been ill. When he heard that the patient had been afflicted for thirty-eight years, Jesus took pity on him and asked, "Do you want to get well?" Although the question seemed self-evident, it implied a forthcoming healing. The man did not answer the question directly, but he obliquely replied that there was no one to help him into the pool when the water was stirred. He said that someone else was always ahead of him.

Because the man did not know Jesus, his reply revealed no faith in him. He avoided answering his question in the affirmative.

Here was a person desperately in need of help and ready to accept any assistance offered to him. Jesus said to the man, "Get up, pick up your mat, and walk!" Suddenly the paralytic felt a power surge through his body. He moved his arms and legs and sat up. Then he stood up, bent over to get his mat, and walked away. Apparently at that moment Jesus disappeared among the crowd.

211

Healed on the Sabbath

The paralytic obeyed Jesus by picking up his mat. With it he walked the streets of Jerusalem on his way home. But he was stopped immediately by Pharisees, who accused him of desecrating the Sabbath. The Scriptures stated explicitly that no one could carry a load on the Sabbath and bring it into the city.

The carrying of a simple mat would hardly qualify as a load, but the Pharisees failed to show any leniency and were restrictive by following the letter of the law. Instead of rejoicing that an invalid had been set free from his long-term bondage and could now worship God on the Sabbath, the Pharisees charged him with breaking the law. They squelched all the joy the man had in being able to walk again.

In his defense, the former paralytic informed his accusers that the one who had healed him told him to take up his mat and walk. And in obedience he had done just that. The Pharisees asked who this person was who ordered him to walk the streets of Jerusalem with a mat. He replied that he did not know, for his benefactor had disappeared and was nowhere to be seen.

Later that day, Jesus met the former invalid walking in the temple area, where he might have gone to praise God. Jesus was interested in healing not only the man's body but also his soul. He said to him, "Look, you have been healed. Don't continue in sin or something worse may happen to you."

Jesus implied that the man's proclivity to sin was of long duration, whatever the sin might have been. Hence he warned him not to continue in sin, which was perhaps the reason for the man having suffered all these years. Should he disobey, something worse might happen to him.

Instead of staying away from the Pharisees, the man went and told them who had healed him. Possibly he wanted to acquaint them with Jesus' supernatural healing power. The negative effect, however, was that this information made it increasingly difficult for Jesus to do the work to which the Father had sent him.

Points to Ponder

- As we witness for Jesus, we do well to be wise as serpents and harmless as doves. The evil one is ready to take advantage of us when we speak on behalf of the Lord. Our prayer should be that God may grant us the gift of the Spirit to speak through us. We must be his mouthpiece guided by his Word and Spirit.
- Not every sickness can be traced to sin. If that were true, Job's so-called friends would have been correct in their counsel. God often uses sickness for his purposes, and that includes drawing us closer to him.
- As much as possible, we should keep the Lord's Day free from nonessential work so we can devote ourselves to worship and beneficial activities that glorify God. On the other hand, we should refrain from being legalistic and loveless in our attitudes toward others.
- In the Gospels, Jesus shows us how to celebrate the day of rest properly, namely, by doing that which pleases God. We are to live not for ourselves but for him. Every time we come together to worship God, we should remember that he is the host and we are the guest. He speaks to us through his Word and the pastor's sermon, and we respond to him in prayer and song. Worship, therefore, is always a conversation of two parties.

213

MIRACLES AND JESUS

THE VIRGIN BIRTH

Matthew 1:18–25; Luke 1:26–38

Scriptural Evidence

The miracles that Jesus performed on this earth during his active ministry differ from those that touch on his birth, transfiguration, resurrection, and ascension. Jesus was active in healing people, even raising them from the dead. With respect to his beginning and eventual departure (not to overlook his transfiguration and resurrection), the miracles that occurred were done *to* him rather than *by* him. These phenomena are God's intervention evident in every instance. The stark reality is that these miracles simply cannot be understood to anyone's satisfaction without a degree of spiritual insight.

The entire Christian church confesses the virgin birth of Jesus in worship services, especially during the Christmas celebration. His birth recorded in the Gospels can never be explained scientifically. True, the biological fact is that human beings are born out of the union of a man and a woman. But Jesus was born of the Virgin Mary who, as the Bible states, was overshadowed by the Holy Spirit.

217

The angel Gabriel first came to a priest named Zechariah, who with his wife, Elizabeth, were advanced in age and childless. The angel told the priest that his wife would bear a son, whom they were to call John. In due time the child was born—in itself a miracle. John became the forerunner and way-preparer for Jesus.

Half a year later Gabriel visited Mary, who as a young teenager and a virgin was promised in marriage to Joseph. The angel called her highly favored in the sight of God because she would give birth to a son, whom she was to call *Jesus*. This child would be the Son of God and rule over a kingdom that would never end.

Mary asked the angel how this would happen because she was a virgin and not yet married. The answer she received was this: "The Holy Spirit will come upon you, and the power of the Most High will overshadow you. So the child to be born will be holy and called the Son of God."

When Joseph, her future husband, heard about Mary's pregnancy, he wanted to break off his relationship with her. But an angel of the Lord told him that the matter was of God and that he should take Mary as his wife into his home. He had no sexual relations with her during her pregnancy. When the child was born, they named him Jesus.

The Gospels present the account of Jesus's virgin birth in relatively few verses. They convey the matter as a divine mystery that cannot be explained rationally. With our limited understanding of God bringing about the virgin birth of Jesus, we do well to admit that no human being can fully clarify God's mysteries.

Denial

Modern scholars approach the biblical text and state that the account of Jesus's birth must be reinterpreted. They say that the story simply does not rest on logical facts. It is scientifically impossible to have a child born without human intercourse. It is a fact of life that fertilization calls for the interaction of a male and a female.

Two thousand years ago, these scholars claim, people in a Middle Eastern culture might believe a myth about the birth of Jesus. In that culture, his followers regarded him as the second Adam. Just as the first Adam was created without a father and a mother, so the second Adam, Jesus, was portrayed as being born without the intervention of a human father.

In the early stages of Christianity, so these scholars say, the people expressed themselves in religious concepts and terms current in that day. Symbols were used to communicate reality without factual history. Rather, legends and myths were part of the culture of that day. Now in modern times, these signs and symbols are no longer appropriate. They must be reinterpreted to be made meaningful for the people of today.

Mythological presentations of religious truth that were acceptable in ancient times must now be stripped of all the accretions that have accumulated in times past. When the extra layers have been removed, so say modern scholars, the people can begin to appreciate the message. For them, with regard to the birth of Jesus, the simple message is that he was born through the sexual union of his father, Joseph, and his mother, Mary. In short, the mystery of the first century has now been converted into the reality of human procreation.

Early Church

Did Jesus's followers in the first century fail to preserve an objective picture of reality? The answer is that the early church presented a message that was based on factual history. Luke, the writer of the third Gospel, states unequivocally that he carefully investigated everything from the beginning by listening to those who were eyewitnesses and ministers of the Word, and that included Mary, Jesus's mother. Luke wrote an accurate and orderly account of the things that had been fulfilled among these eyewitnesses. They precisely stated what had happened and how God worked out the mystery of Jesus's birth.

In their respective Gospels, both Matthew and Luke relate the same factual material. They express total unanimity in regard to the conception and birth of Christ. Although they present two different accounts, they exhibit complete harmony related to essential points in the story.

We admit that stories of virgin births circulated in the ancient world, but these fables cannot compare with the simplicity of the Gospel accounts. The Christians already adopted, near the end of the first century, a creedal statement with the simple wording that Jesus was born of the Virgin Mary. Immediately following the time when these Gospels were written, Jesus's virgin birth was accepted as part of the apostolic doctrine. Similarly, the early church fathers during the second and third centuries regarded this tenet as a basic part of the Christian faith.

These church fathers never questioned the supernatural birth of Christ. For them it was not a new doctrine that the church had formulated in the second half of the first century. The passing on of factual material was still done orally by people who remembered the teachings of the apostles. For instance, the apostle John lived to about AD 98, and Papias, one of his disciples, wrote that he would rather listen to the voice of a living witness than to read these teachings on paper.

The so-called Apostles' Creed plainly states that Jesus "was conceived by the Holy Spirit, born of the Virgin Mary." The church accepted as a principle of faith Christ's supernatural birth. Because of that birth, Christians acknowledged Jesus' sinless life and described him as the Savior of the world. If

Joseph had been his human father, Jesus would never have been able to take away the sin of the world.

Those people who deny the miracle of Jesus's virgin birth also reject the miracles he performed. They find it impossible to believe that he walked on the water of the Lake of Galilee, fed crowds of four thousand and five thousand people, and brought back to life a man who had been dead for four days. They also deny the resurrection of Jesus by stating that he died on the cross and subsequently was buried outside the walls of Jerusalem. They consider Jesus an ordinary man who, because of his opposition to Rome and the Jewish religious authorities of his day, received the death penalty, but he never rose from the dead.

By contrast, the early Christians regarded Jesus as the Son of God, who because of his divine nature performed miracles, died on the cross, was buried, and rose again on the third day by the power of God. The early Christians accepted the Gospel account as verifiable truth that tolerated no denials. For them, the good news was God's Word, and they confessed Jesus as God's messenger.

For two millennia the church has accepted and believed the Scriptures as God's inspired, infallible Word. These Scriptures are called *The Holy Bible*, which means it originated with God. The term *holy* signifies that he set it apart from other books and sanctified it. All Scripture is God-breathed and God-inspired and belongs to him.

In fact, in the last few verses of the Bible we read God's copyright. He warns the reader not to add anything to it or to take away anything from this book of prophecy.

Points to Ponder

- Matthew presents Jesus's genealogy in which he lists Joseph as the legal father of Jesus. Luke adds an explanatory note to his version of this genealogy

221

and says, "Jesus . . . was the son (as was thought) of Joseph."

- The name *Jesus* is the equivalent of *Joshua* in the Old Testament. The word means "the Lord is salvation" or "the Lord helps." The angel of the Lord who appeared to Joseph explained the name *Jesus* by saying, "He shall save his people from their sins."

- Mary's faith in God is exemplary. She believed the angel Gabriel and offered herself in obedience to God. She was aware of the shame and humiliation that her pregnancy would bring to her in Jewish society. Yet she composed a magnificent hymn about her child to be born. In that song she glorifies the Lord God and honors his name.

- In their respective Gospels, both Matthew and Luke report that Jesus is the Son of the Most High God. Although their accounts of Jesus's birth differ in regard to perspectives, both share common details. It is indeed remarkable that there is not even a trace of contradiction in them. Luke writes that his account of the things that have happened has been completely fulfilled. That is, the report is both trustworthy and accepted as established truth.

THE TRANSFIGURATION

Matthew 17:1–8; Mark 9:2–8; Luke 9:28–36

Heavenly Glory

A week before his transfiguration, Jesus had told the disciples about his death and resurrection. But his followers, especially Peter, had difficulty understanding the meaning of this prediction. In effect, Peter had rebuked Jesus by saying that this should never be allowed to happen. He could not see their teacher suffer and die in Jerusalem.

Eight days later Jesus took three of his disciples—Peter, James, and John—up to Mount Hermon, leaving the other nine behind at the foot of the mountain. He needed privacy for prayer and fellowship with his Father. He knew that in the near future he would face trial and execution in Jerusalem, and therefore he asked God for strength and encouragement.

While Jesus was praying, the appearance of his face changed completely, shining like the sun, and his clothes became brilliantly white—so bright that no laundry detergent could get them any whiter. Then Moses and Elijah came and talked with Jesus, appearing as Old Testament saints translated to heaven in bygone eras.

These two men appeared in glorious splendor to talk with Jesus about his imminent departure from this earth. This departure would happen in Jerusalem. They were sent by God to strengthen and encourage him for the task that lay ahead of bringing the work of salvation to completion.

The evangelist Luke reports that the three disciples were overcome by sleep. Peter and his companions awoke and saw the glory of heaven that surrounded Jesus and the two glorified saints standing there with him. Here heaven was brought down to earth by God's power. This was a miracle in itself, that mortal men were allowed to see a glimpse of heaven's glory.

Jesus's disciples were human beings with earthly minds, unaccustomed to the blinding light that radiated from Jesus and his visitors. Peter, who often spoke when he should have kept quiet, made a foolish remark. He addressed Jesus saying: "Master, it is good to be here. Let's make three shelters—one for you, one for Moses, and one for Elijah." Luke adds the sobering comment, "He didn't know what he was saying." Perhaps because of lingering sleepiness, Peter was unable to think straight. We can well imagine that the disciples were scared and confused in the presence of these glorified men.

The essence of Peter's remark was an attempt to keep heaven on earth. But common sense would have told him that heavenly beings residing in glorious splendor might not want to dwell on earth in makeshift tents. Where would he get the material to construct these temporary dwellings? Why only three tents when there were six people? It would have been better if he had focused his attention on heavenly matters instead of earthly things.

A Heavenly Voice

Then a bright cloud overshadowed them while Jesus and his heavenly visitors continued their conversation. This was God's glory cloud that in earlier days had descended on the tabernacle when it was dedicated. And this same cloud filled the temple of Solomon when God entered the Holy of Holies. This cloud represented God's presence on earth.

Then the voice of God the Father spoke out of the cloud and said, "This is my beloved Son in whom I am well pleased. Listen to him." God's voice testified to the divinity of Jesus; these were the same words God spoke when Jesus was baptized in the River Jordan.

God affirmed his love for the Son by mentioning his pleasure in the Son's willingness and obedience to go to the cross. Not only the two visitors from heaven talked about Jesus's departure, but God the Father also made known his satisfaction that the Son would fulfill his task on earth, namely, to die for his people. Jesus was now ready to go to Jerusalem and face suffering and death.

Decades later Peter reminisced on this unforgettable experience and wrote about Jesus receiving glory and honor from God the Father. He reiterated the very words conveyed to him by the Majestic Glory, that is, God who spoke from the cloud: "This is my beloved Son, with him I am well pleased" (2 Peter 1:16–18). Peter did not have to rely on a written document, for these words were indelibly recorded in his memory. He had experienced a view of heaven that guided him while on earth and gave him a longing to be with Christ in heaven.

When the voice from the cloud spoke, the disciples were scared to death and fell with their faces to the ground. But Jesus came to them and said, "Get up and don't be afraid." They looked up and saw only him, for the heavenly visitors had left.

Jesus was transfigured in the presence of his disciples, who were permitted to see a glimpse of heaven. This transformation could be observed externally, namely, Jesus took on the appearance of heavenly glory that he had prior to becoming a human being. In a sense, Moses earlier experienced the same transfiguration on top of Mount Sinai in God's presence when his face was shining with glory light. We read the account of Jesus's transfiguration in the Gospels, but we cannot explain his transforming glory similar to that of Moses and Elijah.

As they walked down the mountain, the three disciples were overcome by the experience of witnessing heavenly glory. Jesus gave them strict instructions not to talk to anyone about this event until he had risen from the dead. His word was not clear to them, and they were puzzled about what he meant by the reference to his resurrection.

The conversation Moses and Elijah had with Jesus centered on his departure from this earth. The stark truth was that Jesus would suffer and die in Jerusalem. Then Jesus plainly told the three disciples that he would rise again from the dead.

The significance of Jesus's forthcoming departure meant that he would die a cruel death on a cross with the objective that his people would be set free from the burden of sin and guilt. The Book of Revelation discloses that the saints in heaven rejoiced when Jesus accomplished that feat. It meant Satan's defeat and his eventual banishment to the lake of fire.

Jesus informed the three disciples about his resurrection from the dead. Although they did not understand the meaning of these words, he signified that on the third day after dying on the cross he would rise from the grave.

Points to Ponder

- Moses and Elijah are two symbolic figures who represent the Law and the Prophets, namely, two parts of the Old Testament Scriptures. Jesus as the Son of God embodies the New Testament. And his transfiguration account is a depiction of the entire Word of God.

- Jesus came to this earth to live and die for sinners; we are on this earth to live and die for Christ. Jesus was transfigured and gave his disciples a glimpse of heaven; we look forward to Jesus's return to be transformed in a moment, in the twinkling of an eye. Then we will be clothed with immortality and with that which is imperishable. When Jesus comes back, we shall be with him eternally.
- The last book of the Bible, Revelation, permits us a glimpse of heaven. The New Jerusalem as the Holy City shall come down to earth. God will be forever with his people and be their God. He will wipe away every tear from their eyes, death will be banished, crying and grief will have ended, and pain will be no more.

THE RESURRECTION

Matthew 28:1–8; Mark 16:1–8;
Luke 24:1–10; John 20:1–8

Raised from the Dead

During his ministry, Jesus raised three people from the dead. They were the young man of Nain, the daughter of Jairus, and Lazarus. These people returned to life, and in the case of Lazarus it was after being in the grave for four days. Jesus called him back to life so that he could make the family circle complete again. But these three people raised from the dead eventually had to face death again after some years had elapsed. They were mortal like all human beings and would have to die yet again.

When Jesus died on the cross that Friday afternoon at three o'clock, an earthquake struck the city of Jerusalem and rocks split. Then something miraculous happened. The tombs outside the city were opened, and many of the bodies of holy people who had been buried came back to life. These resurrected people walked around in the city after Jesus's resurrection Sunday morning and were witnesses to many people. We assume that they did not die again but after their appearing were taken up body and soul to heaven.

The resurrection of these holy people is a promise to all of us that we too will arise from the dead at the time of Jesus's return. Then death will lose its power, and the angel of death as the last enemy will be cast into the lake of fire. There Satan, the beast, the false prophet, and their followers will be spending eternity. By contrast, God's people will live eternally in heavenly glory with Jesus in the presence of God.

Jesus's Resurrection

From late Friday afternoon until early Sunday morning, Jesus's body lay in the tomb of Joseph of Arimathea outside the walls of Jerusalem. Early that morning another earthquake shook the city, and Jesus came forth from the tomb and left. As witnesses to his resurrection, two angels were stationed at the place where his body had lain. They were the ones who addressed the women who came to minister to Jesus's body. They told the women that Jesus was not in the grave but that he had risen from the dead.

The large stone that had sealed the entrance to the tomb was rolled away as if it were as light as the weight of a brick. How did Jesus leave his confinement? At his resurrection he was no longer bound by the laws of time and space. When he was born in Bethlehem, Joseph registered his birth at the city hall, and he became a citizen in Israel. When he died Friday afternoon outside Jerusalem, the city clerk registered Jesus of Nazareth as deceased. He was no longer a citizen on earth but a citizen of heaven. As a heavenly being with a glorified human body, he now could enter a room with locked doors and depart at will. Hence a tomb could no longer hold him prisoner. Jesus arose from the grave as Victor over death and hell.

No theory of Jesus having swooned on the cross and in the coolness of the tomb revived can receive support from the historical facts. The spear wound in his side emitted blood and water, which is a sign of death.

The Jewish leaders paid the soldiers top money for spreading the story that while they slept the disciples came to steal Jesus's body. But the truth of the matter is that at the moment of Jesus's resurrection, the soldiers were scared stiff. Here is the turn around: those who guarded the tomb of a dead man were like dead men when he appeared alive.

The story of Jesus's disciples having stolen his body in the middle of the night is contradicted by the fact that his grave clothes were neatly folded. This would not be the case if they had hurriedly taken the body. In addition, the fabricated story about stealing the body of Jesus proves in itself that the tomb was empty. If the tomb had not been empty, there would be no resurrection account and no gospel, and we of all people would be most miserable, as the apostle Paul writes in one of his letters.

The entire New Testament—Gospels, Acts, Epistles, and Revelation—testifies to Jesus's physical resurrection. This good news is foundational to the church universal, for without it the church cannot exist. This proclamation speaks of Christ's triumph over death, and it provides the assurance that all believers share in that resurrection. The good news in a nutshell is this:

- Christ died for our sins.
- He was buried.
- He rose on the third day.
- He appeared to his disciples.

At Jesus's birth, angels were present to announce good tidings; at his resurrection, there were angels telling the women that Jesus had risen from the dead. Angels were God's messengers to proclaim that his plan of salvation had now become reality. Jesus is alive, and so are we in him.

Points to Ponder

- We readily admit that a human being who died and was buried for three days simply cannot rise from the grave. When medical authorities determine that death has taken a person's life, there is no way they are able to resuscitate the deceased. But God is the active subject who raised Jesus from the dead. God is the agent and Jesus the subject.
- The account of a dead person receiving eternal life, so as to never die again, is absurd to countless people. To them death means over and out. Yet Jesus conquered the greatest power on earth, namely death, and he arose from the grave to live eternally.
- Of world religions, only Christianity teaches a complete doctrine of the resurrection. The founders of all other religions died. But the founder of Christianity died and was raised to life. He teaches us that just as he was raised so we too shall rise body and soul to have eternal life and be with him forever.

POSTRESURRECTION APPEARANCES

Matthew 28; Mark 16; Luke 24; John 20—21; Acts 1

Women

Jesus was seen by many people at different times over a period of forty days between his resurrection and his ascension. These physical appearances during which he ate and drank with his people were convincing proofs of being alive. Women received the honor of being the first to learn that Jesus had risen from the dead.

At Jesus's cross women were present to witness his suffering and death, while his disciples—except John—stayed away. At the break of dawn on the first day of the week, women went to the tomb with spices to prepare Jesus's body. They were the first ones to witness his resurrection. They met the angels, heard the good news, and received the instruction that Jesus would meet his disciples in Galilee. The women were the ones who reported the news to the disciples and to Peter.

One person who saw him on that first day was Mary Magdalene, who had been set free from demon possession and in her gratitude supported Jesus financially. She was devoted to him; she was present at the cross and three days later at the tomb. When she saw the stone removed from the entrance to the tomb, she ran to Peter and John and told them that Jesus's body was not there. Then she returned to the garden area outside the tomb and wept.

Once again she approached the tomb and looked inside. She saw two angels, one seated at the place where Jesus's body had lain and the other where his feet had been. They asked her why she was crying. She replied that her Lord had been taken away but she did not know where they had put him.

Mary Magdalene noticed someone standing next to her who also asked why she was weeping and whom she was looking for. She thought that the man was the gardener. But when she heard Jesus's voice calling her by name, she recognized him and was filled with joy. She cried out, "Teacher." Then she bowed down on her knees and put her arms around his feet as if to keep him near her.

But Jesus made it known to her that a change had taken place. His earthly life had come to an end at the cross. His transformed body no longer hampered by time and space would ascend to his Father. He instructed Mary to tell the disciples, whom he now called brothers, that he would return to his Father and their Father, to his God and their God.

Jesus' sonship is different from the sonship of his followers. He is the unique Son of God by nature, while we are sons and daughters by adoption. Although there is a difference, the intimacy of the Father to his people remains. God is Father to his Son and to the broader family of his adopted children.

Two at Emmaus

During the course of the afternoon that Easter Sunday, two people—a husband called Cleopas and his unnamed wife—were walking from Jerusalem to their home in the village of Emmaus, a distance of about seven miles (eleven kilometers). They would be able to reach their destination in about two and a half hours.

As they ambled along, they were intensely discussing what they had heard about the crucified Jesus who, according to reports, had arisen from the dead. They were so involved in this topic that they had not noticed the presence of a stranger who was walking next to them. He could not help overhearing their conversation and thus asked what they were discussing.

Cleopas and his wife stopped and in amazement asked whether the stranger was a visitor to Jerusalem, unacquainted with the news of the day. He wanted to know what that news was. They told him that it concerned Jesus of Nazareth, whom they regarded as a prophet. But the chief priests had arrested him, and the Romans had sentenced him to a cruel death on a cross. The couple said that they were sorely disappointed because they saw Jesus as a leader who could set them free from Roman oppression.

The couple continued to tell the stranger that in the early morning hours some women had gone to the tomb where Jesus was buried and were told by angels that he was alive. Also others had gone there and came back with the news that the report of the women was true.

Then the stranger began to talk and called them foolish for not believing what the prophets had said about the sufferings the Christ had to endure. He revealed that he had a thorough knowledge of the Scriptures. He began with the books of Moses and from there went to those of the prophets and taught them what was said about the Christ.

As they approached the village of Emmaus, the day was spent. The husband and wife showed hospitality to the stranger by inviting him to their home for a meal and lodging. He accepted their kindness, and as the wife prepared dinner, the men continued their discussion. When the meal was ready and they were seated at the table, the guest took the bread and prayed a prayer of thanksgiving. Then he broke the bread and gave it to the husband and his wife. At that moment they suddenly realized that their guest was Jesus, who then mysteriously vanished from their sight.

How did Cleopas and his wife recognize Jesus?

- Did they see the nail marks in his hands?
- Was it the breaking of the bread?
- Could it be the prayer he offered?
- Did the guest function as their host?

They realized that their risen Lord had visited their home. Their hearts were bursting with excitement. They had to share the news with others, so they hurried back to Jerusalem and to the upper room where the disciples were staying.

Before they could share their news, the others excitedly told them that Jesus had appeared to Simon Peter and that he had risen indeed. Then they were given a chance to tell their story. Indeed, there was now no question about the reality of Jesus's resurrection.

Disciples

Jesus appeared to Peter on Easter Sunday morning, but the evangelists provide no details about that meeting. He came to the upper room that evening and entered even though the disciples had locked the doors for their own security. But Jesus could not be barred, for his transformed body went straight through walls and doors. He met with his disciples and the two from Emmaus who were with them. Of the disciples, there were only ten. Thomas was not with them, for he refused to believe that Jesus had risen from the dead, and Judas had hung himself.

235

Jesus addressed them with the common greeting that is still used among Jews today, "Peace to you." Even though the disciples had elatedly talked about Jesus's appearances, they were still astonished and frightened when they suddenly saw him in their midst. Was he for real, or was he a ghost?

Jesus showed the disciples the scars in his hands, feet, and side. He calmed their fears by inviting them to touch him. When they still were surprised, he asked them for something to eat to prove that he had a body of flesh and bones. When they gave him a piece of broiled fish, they realized that they were not seeing a ghost but the risen Christ.

Then the disciples were overjoyed that Jesus was back in their midst. Yet something had changed, for his body although restored was different. It had transcending qualities that allowed him to go unhindered to any place and then disappear again. His voice and mannerisms were still the same, but there was something heavenly about him.

Jesus made it known that he had to return to his Father and that the Holy Spirit would come upon them, which indeed occurred seven weeks later. As the Father had sent him to come to this earth, so now Jesus was sending forth his disciples to be his witnesses. Jesus would be in heaven, but the Spirit would dwell on earth in the hearts and lives of God's people.

Exactly one week later, Jesus once more met his disciples in the upper room. Thomas was with them because the others had informed him that they had seen the Lord. But he said that he would not believe the news unless he could see the nail marks in Jesus's hands and the scar of the spear in his side.

Then suddenly Jesus stood in their midst, even though the doors were locked. Again he greeted them with the familiar words, "Peace to you." Then he addressed Thomas as if he had heard his skeptical comments. He asked him to touch the scars on his hands and side with his finger. When Thomas did so, Jesus told him to stop doubting and believe. Doubting Thomas became a believer and uttered the words, "My Lord and my God." He now realized that Jesus wanted him to be his witness in places and countries that needed to hear the gospel. Indeed Thomas became the apostle to the people in India. There the church still bears his name: the Church of St. Thomas.

Points to Ponder

- We are living in a three-dimensional world of height, breadth, and width. But there are additional dimensions that are invisible. Angels exist and so do demons, yet we are unable to see them.
- "Seeing is believing" is a common saying uttered when we see proof of something we doubted at first. But believing in that which is unseen is genuine faith. The apostle Paul says that what we see is temporary but what we do not see is eternal.
- A pastor friend once told me that he visited one of his parishioners who was hospitalized and in a coma. But when the pastor came to the bedside, the man was awake and alert. He said, "Pastor, I have just been to heaven." The pastor was skeptical and asked, "John, how do you know you were in heaven?" John answered, "I saw Jesus." The pastor was still unconvinced and queried, "How do you know it was Jesus?" John replied, "I saw the nail marks in his hands." Then the pastor was satisfied and asked his last question, "What did Jesus say to you, John?" His answer was, "Jesus said, 'I paid for you, John, come.'" Soon afterward John passed away.

THE ASCENSION

Luke 24:50–53; Acts 1:1–11

After Forty Days

The forty days between Easter and the ascension are marked by Jesus's numerous appearances. He was seen by his disciples but also by his half brother James, who in later years became the head of the Jerusalem church, presided at the Jerusalem Council, and wrote a letter that is part of the New Testament. Also, Jesus appeared to over five hundred people at one time, many of whom were still alive when Paul wrote his first letter to the Corinthians some twenty-five years later.

The appearances of Jesus happened during a forty-day period, but his teaching ministry came to an end on the day of his ascension. Jesus concluded his earthly ministry when he ascended to take his place at the right hand of God the Father in heaven. From there he would appear to the apostles in visions to give them instructions. For instance, he directed Paul to stay in Corinth, saying that he had many people in that city. And he revealed that Paul had to testify for him in Jerusalem and also in Rome.

No one can adequately explain Jesus's ascension, because at the moment of his death he ceased to exist as a citizen of this earth. His resurrection put him in the category of heavenly beings, and his ascension must be understood as leaving this earth physically and spiritually taking up permanent residence in heaven. Jesus's ascent to heaven actually began already with his resurrection. The periodic appearances to his people were interruptions of a heavenly stay that became permanent at his ascension. The event itself cannot be explained because Jesus's heavenly existence is veiled from human eyes and ears.

The ascension of Jesus serves as a sign that the relationship with his disciples changed from his being physically present to being spiritually accessible. From heaven he now rules supreme, receives prayers and petitions offered in his name, and intercedes for us to God the Father. His ascension brings to a close his earthly presence and ushers in his triumphal entry into heaven as angels, authorities, and powers are in submission to him. These include those that are the spiritual forces of evil, including Satan. Christ Jesus is the supreme ruler in heaven and on earth.

Concluding Reflections

After Jesus ascended to heaven, two angels sent by God stood next to the disciples, who were gazing into the sky. The angels asked the men why they were looking upward. Then they gave them this assurance, "This same Jesus, who has been taken from you into heaven, will come back in just the same way as you have seen him go into heaven." At the time of the consummation when the trumpet sounds and the voice of the archangel is heard, Jesus shall return with power and great glory. Here is a truism: as he ascended so shall he return.

239

Although scientists are unable to verify the miracles of Jesus's birth, resurrection, and ascension, the incontrovertible fact remains that they happened. They are cardinal truths of the Christian faith. God created Adam and Eve, the first human beings, who had no father and no mother. So he brought Jesus into the world born of a virgin without the intrusion of a human male. Also, God raised Jesus Christ from the dead to demonstrate his victory over death and the grave.

With respect to Jesus's birth, transfiguration, resurrection, and ascension, Christians rightly speak of divine intervention and confess that God performed these miracles through the Holy Spirit. They interpret them in the context of faith because from a human perspective no one can explain these phenomena. Intuitively they know that Jesus was born of the Virgin Mary, that he arose physically from the grave on the first Easter Sunday, and that he ascended to heaven.

Points to Ponder

- We have the assurance that as Jesus was glorified so we too will be glorified. The dust of the earth is now on the throne of the majesty on high. That is, God created Adam as the beginning of the human race from dust particles of the earth. Jesus shared in our humanity by assuming our flesh and blood. He arose bodily from the grave, ascended to heaven, and is now seated next to God on the throne.

- Jesus is our advocate at God's right hand to plead our cause to him. The account of Jesus's ascension is therefore a source of comfort and assurance to us. He speaks to the Father in our defense.

- Although we see that the members of Christ's church are oppressed, harassed, persecuted, beaten, raped, tortured, and killed, we know that Jesus is King of kings and Lord of lords. Christ Jesus is the supreme ruler on the face of this world. He will return to take vengeance on his enemies and redeem his people.

- What does Jesus's ascension mean for us? The Bible gives us hope and confidence that we shall be with him where he is, because he has prepared a place for us. Here on earth we learn how to live rightly in preparation for living with Christ eternally in heavenly glory.

FAITH HEALING

HEALING TO AID OUR FAITH

Acts 5:15–16; 19:11–12; James 5:14–16

Healing Is God's Work

James, the half brother of Jesus and writer of the Epistle of James, asks the simple question, "Are any of you sick?" and then provides a definitive answer. He instructs a sick person to call the elders of the church. When they come, the elders should pray in the name of the Lord and anoint the sick person with oil. James asserts that when prayer is offered in faith, the sick person will be restored to robust health.

The elders depend on the Lord to perform the miracle of healing the sick, for in themselves they lack the power to make them well. They should realize that they do not possess a permanent gift to heal all those who are ill. But they should continue to pray and ask God for help in time of need.

What happens when there is no healing? Did the elders lack the necessary faith? Was there sin in the life of the sick person that had not been confessed? That is possible but not necessarily true. God may elect not to heal a person, or he may indicate that a sick person should exercise patience. Sometimes he blesses the doctors, surgeons, equipment, and medicine to restore sick people. At other times, there is no healing at all when God decides to take the sick to their eternal home in heaven. Christians who die in the Lord receive his special blessing.

Consider the apostle Paul, who possessed apostolic power and authority to heal various sick and afflicted people and even raise the dead. But when faithful Epaphroditus came from Philippi to visit Paul in a Roman prison, he became ill and almost died, and the apostle was unable to heal him. Paul admits that he left his dear friend and fellow worker Trophimus sick in Miletus at the time the apostle was taken prisoner to Rome a second time. And he instructed his spiritual son, Timothy, to stop drinking only water but to consume a little bit of wine to counteract stomach problems and other frequent ailments.

If Paul had the gift of healing, he could have eliminated the ailments of his co-workers. But it appears that he was unable to use that gift at times. Healing the physical body is God's work, and Paul knew that he was completely dependent on him.

Paul himself suffered from a malady that he called a thorn in his flesh. Three times he prayed fervently to the Lord to remove this ailment from his body. But the answer he received was, "My grace is sufficient for you, for my power is made perfect in weakness." Even though he had given evidence of apostolic signs with great perseverance among the people in Corinth, the Lord did not heal the malady in Paul's own body.

The Book of Acts reveals that people brought their sick to the apostles and asked them for healing. In Ephesus, sick people would touch one of Paul's handkerchiefs or aprons that he had worn, and they were healed. Peter's shadow fell on the sick as he walked past, and they were healed. The apostles in themselves did not have the power and authority to perform these healing miracles. God empowered them with an extraordinary gift. Acts is an account of early church history. It teaches that the apostles and helpers received the gift of healing as an aid to establish churches.

Apparently when the apostles passed away, miraculous gifts also ceased. This is not to say that God cannot perform miracles today. He certainly does. But it signifies that we as Christians must fervently pray for God's intervention. We boldly come in prayer to his throne to receive mercy and find grace to help us in a time of need.

Prayer Offered in Faith

James writes that a prayer offered in faith by the elders of the church will make a sick person well. What is faith? Do only the elders exercise faith when they pray on behalf of the patient, or do both parties have to display their faith?

Let us discuss these questions one by one. What is faith? Faith is not to trust in our own strength but to rely entirely on God's grace and mercy. Faith means to claim God's promises and petition him to fulfill them. Faith is relying on Christ to make our salvation perfect through his completed work on the cross. Faith is calling on the Holy Spirit to fill us with wisdom, strength, and the ability to do God's will.

Do only the elders exercise faith when they pray on behalf of the patient, or do both parties have to display their faith? Both elders and patient must demonstrate a complete trust in the Lord for physical and spiritual healing. Jesus expects from us a childlike faith in him to effectuate healing. He works through the natural means available: the knowledge of a medical doctor, treatment through medicines and therapy, and patience on the part of the one who is being healed.

If there is hidden sin in the heart of the patient that has not yet been confessed, true confession must be made and, where possible and applicable, restitution. God always forgives a repentant sinner through the blood of Christ.

Everything must be done in proper order: spiritual healing precedes physical healing. Confession cleanses the soul, and physical restoration follows.

Although answers to prayer are at times called miracles, we must admit that these are not the miraculous phenomena displayed in the days of Jesus and the apostles. They are ordinary events that confirm God's grace and demonstrate providence at work in our lives. We humbly acknowledge that miracles seemingly occur outside the ordinary course of events. We confess that only God knows how healing takes place, and we are unable to fathom its mystery.

Scripture teaches that the healing process depends on faith in God, for both the one who prays and the patient for whom prayer is offered. However, when there is no healing, it is highly inappropriate and even damaging to say to the patient that he or she lacked the necessary faith to be healed. It is much better to put our trust in God, for he never puts our faith to shame.

There are a number of instances recorded in the Gospels where Jesus healed a sick person without saying anything about faith. But because the scriptural account is brief and sketchy, we do well to admit that the picture is incomplete.

When we pray in faith, we must be aware that God can send an answer in three different ways. He can reply affirmatively by healing the patient immediately; he may want to exercise our faith by having us patiently wait for him to heal in his time; and his answer may be negative in regard to a patient's forthcoming departure from this earth and entrance to heaven.

Christians who humbly entreat God in faith to heal the sick often see results. This need not happen in a miraculous way; it can also take place through the skill of a physician, the use of modern medication, and the application of therapeutic instruments. In biblical times, olive oil was used for medical purposes. For example, the Samaritan poured wine into the wounds of the helpless man who was lying beside the road half-dead. Wine served as an antiseptic to fight infection; after that he poured oil onto the affected areas as a healing ointment.

In addition, the Old Testament Scriptures prescribed a number of preventative health regulations for the people of Israel in regard to food, cleanliness, and self-discipline. God wanted his people to be healthy and gave them the responsibility to exercise proper physical care for themselves.

When the Israelites traveled through the desert, their clothes and sandals did not wear out, they received food and water on a daily basis, and God took away sickness from among them. He was their provider who protected their physical well-being. God's grateful people expressed their thanks to him.

We likewise thank the Lord for his daily provisions. And we pray that he will remove from us sickness, poor health, and infirmities. However, we have no claim to a permanent gift of healing. Instead, we must give God the glory and honor when healing does occur.

The Faith Healer

A reality check tells us that no faith healer can immediately restore people who are both deaf and mute, who have been blind since birth, and whose limbs are withered. No one is able to raise a dead person back to life. Only Jesus and his apostles performed such signs and wonders in the first century.

A faith healer can pray over and for an afflicted person, but he or she will have to confess that not everyone can be healed. There is the acknowledgment that sickness and suffering may be God's plan to strengthen the spiritual life of the patient.

We are exhorted to pray without ceasing and wait in faith for God to supply the answer. No psychologist can explain the miracle of healing Jesus performed at a distance away from the patient. No faith healer can claim the same healing power Jesus displayed during his ministry. He healed invalids without even seeing and touching them. It is our duty to exercise the power of prayer in faith, for we know that the prayer of a righteous person is powerful and effective.

There is a vast difference between Jesus and a faith healer. Jesus healed people instantaneously, even though his methods were not always the same. We read that a paralytic stood up and walked, dead people came back to life, and a leper was completely restored with all his body parts intact. The healings Jesus performed were indisputably authentic without any hint of trickery or fraud. The restoration of sight, hearing, speech, and mind was genuine and could never be disproved. No faith healer is able to do anything that is similar to the miracles Jesus did.

This is not to say that on the mission field where a satanic presence opposes a missionary at every turn, a miraculous healing never occurs. Missionaries testify that in answer to fervent and repeated prayers, sick persons have been healed not necessarily at once but in stages.

Even in Christianized areas, healings may happen that cannot be explained on the basis of medical knowledge. Physicians are often unable to explain

- how a seriously ill patient recovered rapidly,
- why cancer that was expected to spread went into remission, or
- why a chronic condition suddenly subsided and then disappeared.

We accept in faith that Jesus is still the same as he was during his earthly ministry. He ascended to heaven but gave us the promise that he will be with us until the end of time. Therefore, we may expect him to be the Great Physician and heal those who are sick among us.

We come to God in prayer and plead with him to answer us by granting healing and health. The promise that he heals every disease is still relevant, and we ask him to fulfill it. As we hold him to his word, we experience that he never goes back on what he has told us. He is the one who said, "I am the way, the truth, and the life." And he also said that we may ask him anything in his name and he will do it. That is, as long as our petition glorifies God the Father, promotes his kingdom, and is in harmony with his will, he will hear us.

If we take pleasure in lavishing presents on our children at various occasions, how much more is our heavenly Father ready to grant us good gifts that include health and well-being?

Points to Ponder

- The venerable Heidelberg Catechism of the sixteenth century discusses the Christian's need to pray. It provides this rationale: "Because prayer is the most important part of the thankfulness God requires of us. And also because God gives his grace and Holy Spirit only to those who pray continually and groan inwardly, asking God for these gifts and thanking him for them."
- Prayers for restoration must relate to Christ's redemptive work and the working of the Holy Spirit, so that through prayer God the Father may receive glory and honor.
- In his Epistle, James speaks about prayers that God does not answer. He says that they are those in which you ask with the wrong motives in mind. That is, you present your petitions without reference to glorifying God's name, extending his rule on earth, and doing his will. In other words, all our petitions should be offered in harmony with the petitions Jesus has taught us in the Lord's Prayer.

251

CONCLUSION

The Old Testament prophets Elijah and Elisha performed miracles in nature, raised people from the dead, and healed a Syrian general of leprosy. Correspondingly, Jesus carried out numerous wonders and became known as the Galilean miracle-worker. The public marveled and said that they had never seen anything like it in Israel.

By merely speaking a word, Jesus healed the sick, cast out demons, and raised the dead. Not only Jews but also Gentiles became beneficiaries of Jesus's loving care. Though most of his miracles took place in Galilee, others occurred outside the borders of Israel. The Syro-Phoenician woman rejoiced to see her daughter delivered from demon possession. And a father who brought his epileptic son to Jesus near the foot of Mount Hermon witnessed Jesus's healing ministry.

Gentiles and Jews alike put their faith in Jesus and were richly rewarded. Jesus healed the centurion's servant in Capernaum by merely speaking the word without seeing the patient. Indeed Jesus told the people around him that he had not found such faith among the Jews in Israel. Accordingly, he denounced the Galilean towns of Capernaum, Chorazin, and Bethsaida for their lack of response and unwillingness to repent in spite of all the wonders he had performed among them.

During his earthly ministry, Jesus frequently said to the people that if they had faith as tiny as a mustard seed, they would be able to tell a mountain to be moved and cast into the sea. Obviously, he meant this to be understood figuratively rather than literally. He did not wish to imply that his followers could rearrange the contours of the earth; instead he taught that faith is foundational to overcome life's obstacles. That is, our lives must be filled with confidence to glorify God.

In Old Testament times, God often miraculously intervened in nature. For instance, Moses performed miracles in the process of leading the Israelites out of Egypt. They ranged from turning the waters of Egypt into blood to creating a dry path through the Red Sea for the Israelites to reach the other shore.

Conquering the Promised Land, Joshua made the River Jordan stop its flow so the Israelites could cross to the other side. And he caused the sun to stand still during a battle to occupy the land.

By his prayers, Elijah initiated a drought that lasted three and a half years, and then he prayed again to end it. James refers to Elijah in his Epistle and states that the prayer of a righteous man is powerful and effective.

In the time of the exile, Daniel's three friends were thrown into a blazing furnace and walked around in it unharmed. Similarly, Daniel spent a night in the den of lions and came out unhurt.

During his earthly ministry, Jesus commanded a storm on the Lake of Galilee to stop and the wind to cease. He walked on the waves of that lake and helped Peter to do likewise. He turned some 180 gallons of water into wine as a wedding gift to the bridal couple.

With five little cakes and two small fishes on hand, Jesus fed a crowd of five thousand men, not counting the women and children. Some time later he fed four thousand men in addition to the women and children. He cursed a fig tree that within a day withered and died.

Peter had power to heal by having his shadow fall on the sick as he walked past them. And when sick people merely touched Paul's handkerchiefs or aprons, they were healed and evil spirits came out of them.

The author of Hebrews informs his readers that when the gospel was first proclaimed God added his testimony by signs, wonders, and various miracles. There is no indication that the performance of miracles continued indefinitely. Rather, when the era of the apostles came to an end, miracles in nature appear to have stopped. God's gift of performing miracles was a distinguishing mark of being an apostle. When the gospel was well established and society had come to know Christ, miracles ceased.

God still protects his people from harm and danger, so that many of us can testify to a miraculous intervention in our lives. He may deliver us from some harrowing circumstance whether from nature, danger, or disease.

These phenomena usually refer to our physical well-being or needs. But it is safe to say that the miracles that occurred in the days of Jesus and the apostles no longer happen today. No human being has the power to bring the dead back to life, give sight to someone born blind, make the deaf to hear, walk on the waves of the sea, or command both storm and wind to cease.

Yet Jesus is the same yesterday, today, and in the future. He has given us the assurance that he will be with us until the end of time. Thus, in faith we look to him to guide us day by day, protect us from harm, and heal all our diseases. He will see us through to the end, and at his time, take us up in glory to be with him eternally.

FOR FURTHER STUDY

Dickason, C. Fred. *Angels: Elect and Evil.* Chicago: Moody, 1975.

Dickinson, Robert. *God Does Heal Today.* Carlisle, United Kingdom: Paternoster, 1995.

Gaffin, Richard B., Robert L. Saucy, C. Samuel Storms, and Douglas A. Oss. *Are Miraculous Gifts for Today? Four Views.* Edited by Wayne A. Grudem. Grand Rapids: Zondervan, 1996.

Geivett, R. Douglas, and Gary R. Habermas, eds. *In Defense of Miracles.* Downers Grove, IL: InterVarsity Press, 1997.

Lockyer, Herbert. *All the Miracles of the Bible.* Grand Rapids: Zondervan, 1961.

MacDonald, G. *The Miracles of Our Lord.* Wheaton: Harold Shaw Publishers, 1980.

Melinsky, M. A. H. *Healing Miracles.* London: Mowbray, 1968.

Otto, David. *The Miracles of Jesus.* Nashville: Abingdon, 2000.

Phillips, Richard D. *Mighty to Save: Discovering God's Grace in the Miracles of Jesus.* Phillipsburg: Presbyterian and Reformed, 2001.

Ryrie, C. C. *The Miracles of Our Lord.* Nashville: Nelson, 1984.

Twelftree, G. H. *Jesus the Miracle Worker.* Downers Grove, IL: InterVarsity Press, 1999.

Van Der Loos, H. *The Miracles of Jesus.* Leiden, the Netherlands: Brill, 1965.

Warfield, B. B. *Counterfeit Miracles.* Reprint, Edinburgh, Scotland: Banner of Truth Trust, 1979.

Simon J. Kistemaker was educated at Calvin College, Calvin Theological Seminary, and the Free University of Amsterdam. He was ordained into the ministry of the Christian Reformed Church and served the church in Vernon, British Columbia, Canada.

Kistemaker served the Evangelical Theological Society first as president and then as secretary-treasurer for eighteen years. He has taught at Calvin College, Dordt College, and the Reformed Theological Seminary, where he became professor of New Testament in 1971 and still serves today as professor emeritus.

An internationally recognized lecturer, Kistemaker has written numerous books, including *The Parables*, *The Gospels in Current Study*, *The Conversations of Jesus*, and commentaries in the New Testament Commentary series begun by his predecessor, William Hendriksen. Kistemaker contributed commentaries on Acts, 1 Corinthians, 2 Corinthians, Hebrews, the Epistles of James and John, the Epistles of Peter and Jude, and Revelation. Four of these received the Gold Medallion Award from the Evangelical Christian Publishers Association.